PLAYWORK

Candidate Handbook

NVQ/SVQ and CACHE

LEVEL **2**

Tina Farrow
Valerie Stevens
Susan Stanley

For the 2002 Standards

www.heinemann.co.uk
✓ Free online support
✓ Useful weblinks
✓ 24 hour online ordering

01865 888058

Heinemann

Inspiring generations

Heinemann Educational Publishers
Halley Court, Jordan Hill, Oxford OX2 8EJ
Part of Harcourt Education

Heinemann is the registered trademark of
Harcourt Education Limited

© Tina Farrow, Valerie Stevens and Susan Stanley, 2003

First published 2003

08 07 06 05 04 03
10 9 8 7 6 5 4 3 2 1

British Library Cataloguing in Publication Data is available
from the British Library on request.

ISBN 0 435 45216 9

Typeset by Saxon Graphics Ltd, Derby

Printed in the UK by Scotprint.

Tel: 01865 888058 www.heinemann.co.uk

Contents

Acknowledgements

We would like to thank our husbands, partners and families for their enthusiastic support, and for helping us to sustain our motivation for this book.

We would like to thank our enthusiastic Playwork candidates from New College Nottingham who have given us helpful feedback and comments.

We would like to thank our line manager, who has encouraged and supported us to develop new materials, and our colleagues for their moral support and unfailing sense of humour.

We would also like to thank:
Sue Williams at Homestead out-of-school club for use of her policies and procedures.

Jessica Parr for her help typing out record documentation sheets.

Geraldine Chaffe, a former colleague and co-author of the Playwork NVQ level 3 Tutors' resource file.

Camilla Thomas and Mary James for their guidance, patience with the book and tolerance with our communication problems.

Tina Farrow, Sue Stanley and Valerie Stevens

The authors and publishers would like to thank the following individuals and organisations for permission to reproduce material and photographs:

Gareth Boden pages 6, 12, 39, 60 and 155

Alamy pages 11 and 137

Corbis pages 24 and 36

Haddon Davies pages 30, 55 and 64

British Toy and Hobby Manufacturers Association page 76 (top)

European Standard page 76 (middle)

British Standard page 76 (bottom)

Every effort has been made to contact copyright holders of material reproduced in this book. Any omissions will be rectified in subsequent printings if notice is given to the publishers.

Introduction

Welcome to this handbook for the National Vocational Qualification (NVQ) for the level 2 (revised standards 2002) in Playwork. This handbook is designed to give you guidance and to confirm your good practice in working with children and young people, aged 4–15 years, while facilitating development through play. It is particularly directed towards those embarking on a NVQ level 2 Playwork award.

To be an effective and competent playworker or assistant it is important not only to gain knowledge, skills and understanding about children and young people but also to continually update and improve your practice. This book gives ideas and suggestions to aid you in this role.

Why do an NVQ in Playwork?

It is an exciting time to enter into the field of Playwork as there are increasing opportunities for qualified playworkers at all levels. When advertising jobs for staff in out-of-school care and play centres, employers are beginning to specify the need for their employees to have a recognised qualification in Playwork, such as an NVQ. An NVQ is set as a recognised qualification on the National Framework, and registering bodies are asking for this qualification as part of their criteria. Further, NVQs are nationally recognised, which means that this qualification will be acknowledged in any part of the country.

To undertake an NVQ you will need to register with a centre approved by an awarding body and you will need to follow their guidelines for your award. In order to achieve your NVQ you will need to be working with children and young people in a **play setting**. This means that you will be working while you are training.

Part of the NVQ process involves assessment of your practice in the work place by an experienced playworker who is a qualified assessor. In 'NVQ speak', you will hear your assessor talking about 'being competent'. This means that you have reached the required standards set for assessment of your work in a way that meets the National Occupational Standards for the NVQ in Playwork.

NVQs require their candidates to provide and collect evidence to show that they are competent on more than one occasion in working with children and young people (aged 4–15 years); and that they have the underpinning knowledge to back up their performance by showing an understanding as to what is done and why. The National Standards guide you towards the evidence you need to collect and the level at which competency will be judged.

Evidence will be gathered through three key areas:

    What you need to cover – the range
    What you need to do – the performance criteria
    What you need to know – the knowledge, understanding, values and skills for each unit.

Understanding the NVQ Standards

The structure of all NVQ awards follow the same pattern, and like other NVQs the NVQ in Playwork is made up of units of competence described in the National Standards, which list the things that need to be done in the workplace – these are like the main duties in a job description. Units can be gained over a period of time, like building blocks, towards the whole qualification. Each unit is given a title and a reference letter and number (e.g. PW1) and is divided into elements. Each element describes one distinct aspect of the work performed by the playworker, either a specific task or a specific way of working. Each element also has a number and title (e.g. PW1.1.).

Performance criteria indicate the minimum level of performance you must demonstrate in order to be assessed as competent in each required element of the qualification. The range specifies different circumstances or conditions. You must be able to prove competence in all the different circumstances covered by the range as well as adhering to **relevant laws** and the **requirements of your organisation**. Examples of the range include different types of play opportunities–**physical play**, **cultural play**, **environmental play**, and so on.

Each unit describes all the knowledge, understanding, values and skills that you need so that you can do the elements in the unit successfully. You will need to prove to your assessor that you have this knowledge. These knowledge points are also numbered.

Source: based on material from the *CACHE, NVQ in Playwork Level 2 Candidate Handbook.*

How this book will help you with your NVQ

This book is designed to help you through the NVQ mandatory units and is divided into sections or chapters relating to each of the mandatory units. It gives information and advice to help you examine your practice and provide evidence for your units.

This book is not designed to replace the NVQ standards, but to give you options and ideas to help with your NVQ. Before you undertake the activities in this book you will need to confer with your assessor, who will give you guidance and support.

Features of the book

Throughout this book there are a number of features that are designed to encourage you to build on your own experience and help you to see how theory is put into practice in playwork settings.

Keys to good practice – practical suggestions for promoting good practice in your setting

Active knowledge – activities that help you relate the knowledge in the book to what you do in the workplace

Case Studies – these are 'what if' scenarios designed for you to check your understanding, and to think through possible courses of action

Think about it – activities that give you topics to think about, check out and research

Consolidation – questions to check your understanding and give practice in the kinds of questions your assessor may ask you

End of unit tests – questions at the end of each unit which help test the knowledge you have gained as you read through the book

Key words
Throughout the text you will meet words which are highlighted in **bold.** These words come from the NVQ Standards. They are key words you will be expected to know and understand to achieve your award. The meanings of these words can be found in the glossary at the end of the book (pages 169–73).

Playwork assumptions and values

There are many different play settings serving the needs of their communities in a variety of ways. All have one goal – to provide a safe and stimulating environment, where children and young people can develop as individuals, taking part in a multitude of activities, learning about themselves, others and the environment around them.

Playwork assumptions and values are an important part of the above, and will help you and your colleagues create an environment that children and young people will want to be part of. When working with and providing for children's play a holistic approach, which means looking at the whole picture, needs to be adopted. This approach also needs to be in line with Playwork assumptions and values.

Assumptions

The first assumption is that:

Children's play is freely chosen, personally directed behaviour motivated from within; through play the child explores the world and her or his relationship with it, elaborating all the while a flexible range of responses to the challenges she or he encounters; by playing the child learns and develops as an individual.

The second is that:

Whereas children may play without encouragement or help, adults can, through the provision of an appropriate human and physical environment, significantly enhance opportunities for the child to play creatively and thus develop through play.

In this way the competent Playworker always aims to provide opportunities for the individual child to achieve her or his full potential while being careful not to control the child's direction or choice.

Values

Play opportunities are provided in a number of settings (for example Local Authority, Voluntary or Commercial) for children with a variety of needs, in a complex society diverse in culture and belief; nevertheless, competent Playwork always has the following underlying values:

1 The child must be at the centre of the process; the opportunities provided and the organisation which supports, co-ordinates and manages these should always start with the child's needs and offer sufficient flexibility to meet these.

2 Play should empower children, affirm and support their right to make choices, discover their own solutions, to play and develop at their own pace and in their own way.

3 Whereas Play may sometimes be enriched by the Playworker's participation, adults should always be sensitive to children's needs and never try to control a child's play so long as it remains within safe and acceptable boundaries.

4 Every child has a right to a play environment which stimulates and provides opportunities for risk, challenge and the growth of confidence and self-esteem.

5 The contemporary environment in which many children grow up does not lend itself to safe and creative play; all children have the right to a play environment which is free from hazard, one which ensures physical and personal safety, a setting within which the child ultimately feels physically and personally safe.

6 Every child is an individual and has the right to he respected as such; each child should feel confident that individuality and diversity are valued by the adults who work and play with them.

7 A considerate and caring attitude to individual children and their families is essential to competent Playwork and should be displayed at all times.

8 Prejudice against people with disabilities or who suffer social and economic disadvantage, racism and sexism have no place in an environment which seeks to enhance development through play; adults involved in play should always promote equality of opportunity and access for all children, and seek to develop **anti-discriminatory practice** and positive attitudes to those who are disadvantaged.

9 Play should offer the child opportunities to extend her or his exploration and understanding of the wider world and therefore physical, social and cultural settings beyond their immediate experience.

10 Play is essentially a co-operative activity for children both individually and in groups. Playworkers should always encourage children to be sensitive to the needs of others; in providing play opportunities, they should always seek to work together with children, their parents, colleagues and other professionals and where possible, make their own expertise available to the wider community.

11 Play opportunities should always be provided within the current legislative framework relevant to children's rights, health, safety and well-being.

12 Every child has a right to an environment for play, and such environments must be made accessible to children.

Source: based on material from the *CACHE, NVQ in Playwork Level 2 Candidate Handbook*.

Contribute to positive relationships in the play setting

Unit PW1

The way that a playworker interacts with children, young people and adults should always contribute to **positive relationships**. This unit focuses on how we establish, develop and maintain such relationships in a positive and helpful manner.

This unit is divided into three elements:

- PW1.1 Develop and maintain positive relationships with children and young people.
- PW1.2 Contribute to positive relationships between children/young people and others in the play setting.
- PW1.3 Contribute to positive relationships with parents and carers.

The Play Values covered in this unit are shown below:

Value No	Statement
1	The child must be at the centre of the process.
2	Play should empower a child or young person.
3	Play should be freely chosen and directed by the child or young person within the guidelines of the setting.
6	Every child is an individual and should be respected for who they are.
7	As a playworker, you should be considerate and caring.
8	As a playworker, you should promote equal opportunities for all children and young people in your setting, regardless of ability, race, culture, social background, etc.
9	Within a play setting, you should be a positive role model and create co-operative working.
11	Play opportunities should be provided within the current legislative framework.

As a playworker in a play setting, you will build relationships with a variety of people, including:

- children and young people
- people from other play settings
- community groups
- parents and carers
- scheme managers
- professional groups, e.g. schools, social services and health authorities.

Building good relationships in the play setting will contribute to the quality of the service you provide and improve the experiences of the children and young people.

It will also enhance the reputation of the setting. Parents and carers need to have confidence in the setting, and in the playworkers, before they will feel happy about leaving their children in your care. If they see that the staff work together for the benefit of the children and offer a good quality, safe play environment, they will feel confident that their children are in good hands.

To be an effective playworker, you need to understand the legal framework. This means knowing what you can and cannot do and what you must do in certain situations.

The Children Act (1989) was established to protect children and young people. It sets out clear guidelines to ensure that children and young people are cared for in a welcoming and friendly environment. It details legal requirements for settings where children are cared for, and recommends that regular inspections are carried out to ensure that settings meet the required standard.

The DfES (Department for Education and Skills) National Standards are a baseline for quality below which no provider (the registered person in each registered setting, usually the owner or manager) can fall. The Children Act (1989) requires that providers meet these requirements. An example of a National Standard (Standard 3) is shown below.

Standard 3: Care learning and play

- The registered person meets children's individual needs and promotes their welfare. He or she plans and provides activities and play opportunities to develop children's emotional, physical and intellectual capabilities.
- The registered person and his or her staff listen and value what children say, talk with them about what they are doing and have high expectations of what they can achieve.
- The registered person and his or her staff encourage children to be confident and independent and to develop their self-esteem.

Standard 3 describes the atmosphere and feelings you want to create in a play setting. It is about putting the children and young people's needs first, so that everything the playworker does is to help and benefit the children. This is what empowerment means; children have the right and opportunity to choose what they want to do. They are empowered to make decisions for themselves, rather than being told what to do.

Think about it

Why do you think it is beneficial for children to be empowered?

Should playworkers set out all the activities and decide when the children will use them, or should children be involved in the planning stage and decide what they want to do and when?

Each setting needs to have clear guidelines within its policies regarding confidentiality, and playworkers must read and implement these polices. Below is an example of an out of school club policy.

Homestead out of school club privacy and confidentiality statement

The work undertaken by the out of school club with children and families will sometimes bring us into contact with **confidential information**. To ensure that all those using and working in the club can do so with confidence, we will respect confidentiality in the following ways:

- Parents will have ready access to the files and records of their own children but will not have access to information about any other child.
- Staff will not discuss individual children other than for purposes of planning or the child's management, and then only with the parents/carers of that child.
- Information given by parents/carers to the staff will not be passed on to other adults without permission.
- Issues to do with the employees, whether paid or unpaid, will remain confidential to the people directly involved with making personnel decisions.
- Any anxieties/evidence relating to a child's personal safety will be kept in a confidential file and will not be shared within the out of school club except with the child's key worker and the officer in charge.

The Data Protection Act (1998) states the legal responsibilities of playworkers with regard to written records. It states who can access them and how they are to be stored.

Homestead out of school club: Parental access to records

- The out of school club believes very strongly that information shared between parents and ourselves is a two-way affair.
- Parents/carers are always welcome and will have ready access upon request (of the officer in charge) to the files of their own children, but will not have access to information about any other child.

Some information that you become aware of may be confidential due to its nature, e.g. medical conditions, family issues, criminal records and child protection issues. In all these cases, you would tell only those whom it was absolutely necessary to tell, and even then you may not need to go into details. For example, if a mother had told you that she had been abused as a child you would not pass on this information unless there was a child protection issue with her child; only then would you tell the designated member of staff. However, if you become aware of information that could affect the health and wellbeing of a child or young person it is your legal duty to pass this information on to a relevant person, e.g. the child's key worker or a designated member of staff.

For example, if a child told you that his mum had an evening job and he was left alone at home for four hours every night, you would need to pass this information to the designated member of staff for the child's safety.

> ✓ **ACTIVE KNOWLEDGE**
>
> Look at your setting's policies on confidentiality and access to records and compare them with the Homestead out-of-school club policies. Find out who you should report any concerns to in your setting.

The children and young people who attend your setting will come from a variety of **social and cultural backgrounds**. Whenever you interact with people, whether it be the children and young people in your care, their parents and carers, other staff, other professional bodies or members of the public, the image you portray should always be non-judgemental and anti-discriminatory. You should take positive action to counter discrimination; this will involve identifying and challenging discrimination and being positive in your playwork practice about people's differences.

Your setting will have a policy that will guide you in all areas of equal opportunities. The policy will be based on the DfES National Standard 9.

Standard 9: Equal opportunities
- The registered person and staff actively promote equality of opportunity and anti-discriminatory practice for all children.
- All children and adults are treated with equal concern and the registered person is aware of relevant anti-discriminatory good practice. The registered person promotes equal opportunities with regard to employment, training, admission to the day care and access to the resources, activities and facilities available.

Calverton out-of-school club equal opportunities policy
It is our intention to make our club equally accessible to children and families from all sections of the local and wider community, irrespective of gender, race, social group, religion, family background or disability. In addition, we aim to ensure that all those who wish to be working or volunteer to help in our club have an equal chance to do so.

Your equal opportunities policy will focus on positive and non-judgmental attitudes as shown in the policy above. It will include various sections, such as the following:

- admissions – ensuring that all children are welcome whatever their background, religion, culture or beliefs
- festivals – ensuring that you celebrate a variety of festivals
- the curriculum – providing activities that everyone can take part in
- special needs – ensuring that children with special needs have their individual needs meet, and have access to facilities, activities and play opportunities

- food – if snacks are required, information should be provided by parents about any special dietary requirements, preferences or allergies the child may have.

It is important that you implement your equal opportunity policy at all times. A welcoming and friendly atmosphere is a major requirement. You should provide a range of equipment and materials that reflect the children's backgrounds and cultures. For example, if you are setting out a painting activity for the children to paint self-portraits, ensure that you have the appropriate paints for all skin colours.

Providing a range of equipment which children can relate to will help them become confident and at ease in the setting. Every child is unique. His or her experiences, and the opportunities he or she has had, often affect play and relationship-building within the setting. By helping children and young people to feel at ease and welcome, you will help develop their interactive skills both socially and as they communicate. This will enhance your relationship with them.

Some of the children and young people who attend your setting may have particular needs. These could be:

- physical needs, e.g. mobility, sight impairment
- social and emotional needs, e.g. lacking in social skills, very emotional
- challenging behaviour, e.g. unable to keep to socially acceptable behaviour.

A particular need might affect a child's ability to play and to build relationships. You should help build each child's confidence and social skills to better enable him or her to integrate and take a full and active part in all the activities and opportunities available. All settings should provide inclusive experiences for children and young people, and this can be done by:

- providing all children with a range of activities with regard to their individual needs
- providing an appropriate **play environment** that meets the individual's needs – all children have the right to develop to their full potential.

CASE STUDY

It is Jack's first session at your setting and you have not met him before. He is 10 years old, has additional needs with regard to his learning, and his carer described him as 'a very shy child'.

1 How you would welcome Jack and support him in the first session?

Develop and maintain positive relationships with children and young people

What you need to learn

- How to welcome children and young people to the setting.
- The communication skills you will need to use.
- How to communicate well with children and young people at different ages.
- Techniques for observing and listening to children.
- The effects of discrimination and how to counter them.

How to welcome children and young people to the setting

It is not only the environment that creates a welcoming and friendly atmosphere, it is also the people who are there. First impressions are important for parents and carers as well as the children and young people. As a playworker, you will need to develop a range of techniques and strategies for interacting with children and young people.

Making eye contact with a child will help her feel welcome

Techniques that you could use when children and young people come to the setting for the first time include the following:

- find out his or her preferred name; be sure you know how to pronounce it, and make an effort to use it
- show him or her around the facility or ask another child to do so. Remember to check that the child knows where the toilets are

- explain any routines that you use
- go over the evacuation procedures in case there is an emergency
- ask him or her if they know any of the children or young people who are already attending
- ask the child if they have any particular interests that you can discuss
- talk to the child and find out what he or she likes to do
- explain any health and safety issues and explain the guidelines for behaviour
- show the child what activities you have available and ask if he or she has played them before
- introduce yourself and the other workers and children
- explain your policy for free play activities
- get the child involved in an activity, and observe him or her during the initial and following sessions to ensure the child is settling in well
- make eye contact when you speak to the child and listen to his or her reply
- try to ask open questions (those that cannot be answered with just yes or no)
- try to be at the same level (bend down for smaller children).

Whatever techniques you adopt, you must ensure that the activities are appropriate for the age and stage of development of the children and young people. Each child and young person is very different and may need to be treated individually, sometimes one-to-one, for example if you have a shy child you may guide them towards a one-to-one activity. You may need to monitor the noise levels in that particular area, and you should observe occasionally throughout the session to ensure that the child is settling in.

The communication skills you will need to use

The way that you communicate with children and young people will be determined by your personal approach. The method you choose will be the most appropriate for the child or young person and suitable for the specific situation. It may take the form of talking and listening or may involve other people, e.g. interpreters.

Keys to good practice: Listening skills

✓ Always listen attentively to what the child or young person is saying.
✓ Look interested and encourage the child to interact with you. It will be of great importance to him or her.
✓ Ask open questions (ones that cannot be answered with yes or no replies).
✓ Find topics of interest to you both.
✓ Use appropriate vocabulary to meet the child's age and stage of development.
✓ Use humour appropriately; do not use sarcasm or put-downs.

Non-verbal communication

Your non-verbal communication, i.e. your gestures, actions and facial expressions, are as important as what you say. Children learn to interpret non-verbal communication at an early age. Think about how your face portrays your feelings.

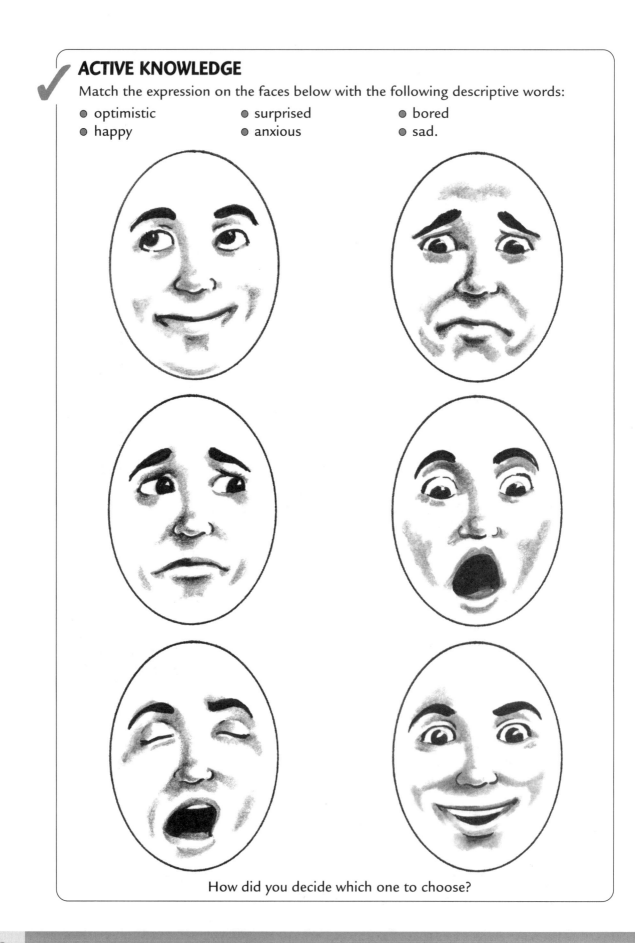

ACTIVE KNOWLEDGE

Match the expression on the faces below with the following descriptive words:

- optimistic
- surprised
- bored
- happy
- anxious
- sad.

How did you decide which one to choose?

It may be that you need to communicate using other methods, e.g. using Makaton. This is a type of sign language where actions mean words or phrases. Some basic Makaton signs are shown below.

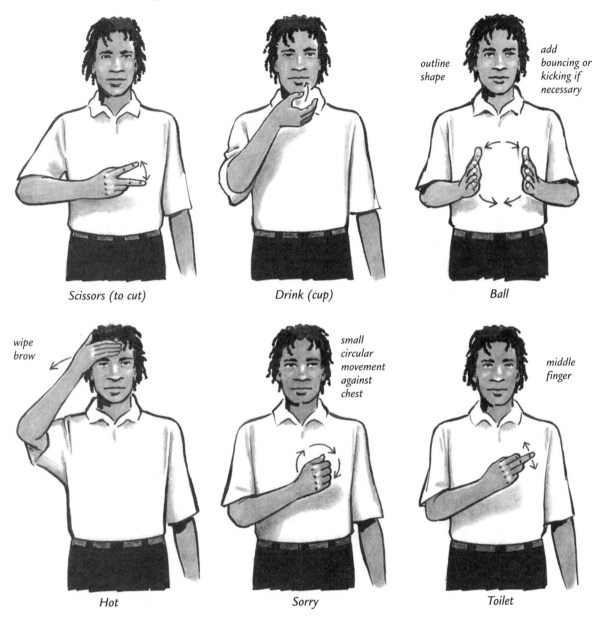

Scissors (to cut) *Drink (cup)* *outline shape* *add bouncing or kicking if necessary* *Ball*

wipe brow *Hot* *small circular movement against chest* *Sorry* *middle finger* *Toilet*

✓ ACTIVE KNOWLEDGE

Research into Makaton signs and learn the one for welcome. Then teach it to the other staff in your setting, and the children and young people.

Learn a song or rhyme in Makaton and teach it to the people in your setting.

Whatever techniques you use, you should ensure that they are at an appropriate level for the child or young person in your care.

How to communicate well with children and young people at different ages

Age/developmental level	Technique
4–7 years	Use language they will understand. Listen carefully, show you are concentrating and interested. Be patient, you may need to explain things more than once. Use eye contact. Have a friendly approach; smile, listen and generally be easy to talk to. Do not assume they will not understand.
8–12 years	Encourage children and young people to express their opinions, ask them what they think and acknowledge their replies. Give explanations to back up what you are saying. Offer opportunities for them to express themselves, e.g. role-play, modelling, painting, drawing, writing. Encourage self-help and independence. Give them responsibilities. Introduce and encourage new vocabulary. Negotiate, listen to their side of disagreements, then come to an amicable agreement. Make time for individual attention. Show patience and understanding.
13–16 years	Find a common interest, e.g. video, music. Challenge stereotypical or racial discrimination, inappropriate terminology and swearing. Negotiate and look for compromises; listen to their reasons. Use humour appropriately; do not use put-downs or sarcasm, laugh at appropriate things, be sympathetic and show empathy. Give them space; use the correct supervision level, do not assume they always want an adult listening in. Treat them like adults; do not patronise or talk down to young people, empower them to express their opinions freely. Use communication to increase their vocabulary, discuss issues as you would with another adult. Use a variety of games to engage them in conversation, e.g. quizzes, board games, etc. Give them responsibility; let them take on regular interesting jobs, e.g. setting out an activity and not just clearing away.

Playworkers need to respond to children as individuals, and by giving respect you receive respect. Children need to feel safe and secure both in the play environment and with the adults who work there.

Makes children feel welcome

Shows you consider their feelings

Boosts self-esteem

Helps develop confidence

Sets a good example

Make time for individual attention

Keys to good practice: Interacting with children and young people

Appropriate behaviour
- ✓ Using correct terminology
- ✓ Responding honestly to questions
- ✓ Listening to problems and concerns
- ✓ Giving space
- ✓ Using appropriate touches

- ✓ Offering options and choices

Inappropriate behaviour
- ✓ Using slang/swear words

- ✓ Discussing own personal problems

- ✓ Sitting an older child on your knee/kissing them
- ✓ Giving advice that contradicts policies

Techniques for observing and listening to children

By listening to children and observing their interactions, playworkers can show that they are interested in the children and value what they say and do. This will give each child a sense of security in the relationship he or she builds with you and will encourage him or her to seek you out to discuss issues and concerns, as well as positive experiences. It will also help you to:

- be aware of developmental delays in language and physical, emotional or social behaviour
- detect problems both within the setting and outside
- identify any health, safety and hygiene issues.

This aspect of a playworker's role will help you develop your skills and understanding of children and young people. Asking questions and giving opinions is a development stage in life. Playworkers are in a useful position to help children and young people develop these skills. The reasons why we should encourage children to ask questions and give opinions are shown below.

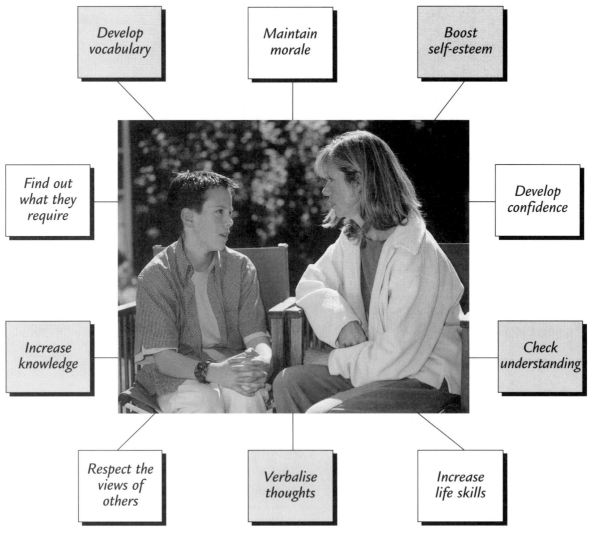

Develop vocabulary

Maintain morale

Boost self-esteem

Find out what they require

Develop confidence

Increase knowledge

Check understanding

Respect the views of others

Verbalise thoughts

Increase life skills

Encourage children to ask questions and give opinions

Different ways of encouraging children and young people to ask questions and express opinions are shown in the table below.

Ways of encouraging questions and expressing opinions	Appropriate responses
Include children and young people in activity planning; set aside time for discussion of ideas.	Act on suggestions and ensure (whenever possible) that activities requested are carried out. Explain rationale for those suggestions not acted upon.
Use every opportunity for talking and discussing, especially at meal times.	Encourage adults to sit with the children in small groups and encourage discussion.
Create a suggestions box.	Check suggestions regularly, discuss ideas and act on them where possible.
Create a children and young people's forum.	Set up a forum, encourage participation and act on suggestions and ideas.
Be non-judgemental.	Offer alternatives rather than set advice; show unconditional acceptance to children and young people, and their families.

Encouraging children to ask questions and express opinions helps to show children and young people that they are valued. If a playworker were to ignore a child or young person and not follow up their ideas and opinions, the child would feel undervalued, and this could affect their self-confidence and esteem. They could then withdraw from making further suggestions.

CASE STUDY

Ahmel is 9 years old. She comes to the play scheme with her mother, who is enquiring about the scheme. Your supervisor asks you to show Ahmel and her mother around the setting and introduce Ahmel to some of the children.

1 What aspects of the setting would you show Ahmel and her mother first?
2 Who would you introduce Ahmel to?

The effects of discrimination and how to counter them

Discrimination is when one particular group or individual is treated unfairly. Anti-discriminatory practice in your setting is very important for the following reasons:

- it sets a good example
- it creates a comfortable atmosphere
- it encourages children to see themselves and others as individuals
- it is necessary to abide by the polices of the setting
- the Human Rights Act (1998) requires it
- it will stop children feeling singled out
- it may boost self-esteem
- it helps children to respect one another
- it ensures everyone has the opportunity to enjoy themselves

- it ensures equal opportunities
- it ensures that children do not feel excluded.

The harmful effects that discrimination can have on children include the following:

- it makes them feel unwanted
- it creates low self-esteem
- they feel different and singled out
- they may become angry and aggressive
- they may become withdrawn
- they may feel isolated or inadequate
- it may encourage unwanted behaviour.

The ways to counteract different types of discrimination are shown in the table below.

Discrimination	Action to counteract it
Boys will not allow girls to play football.	Challenge the boys, explain why girls should be allowed to play, and then select mixed gender teams.
Boys are not allowed to dress up in girl's clothes and vice versa.	Explain that all children benefit from being allowed to participate in role play.
Only celebrating Christian festivals.	Research festivals, ask people from different cultures/religions for advice.
Child being teased because they cannot afford designer clothing.	Stop teasing immediately. Deal with the issue as a group. Explain how clothes don't make the person.
Child who wears glasses being unable to participate in sports.	Adapt equipment and rules for children if necessary.
Children using inappropriate language to describe homosexuality.	Challenge immediately, and follow up with an explanation about how offensive that type of language can be. If necessary give correct terminology.

CASE STUDY

1 Imagine you work at a summer play scheme in a community centre and a young person of about 12 years old comes and looks through the window. You have a group of young people who are playing pool, table tennis, listening to music, playing board games, etc. You glance across 10 minutes later and he is still there. He then appears at the door and asks what you are doing. Describe the actions you would take and the interaction that would occur.

2 Look at the pictures on page 15 and state when you would have intervened and why.

Discuss the strategies you would use to deal with the victim as well as the situation itself.

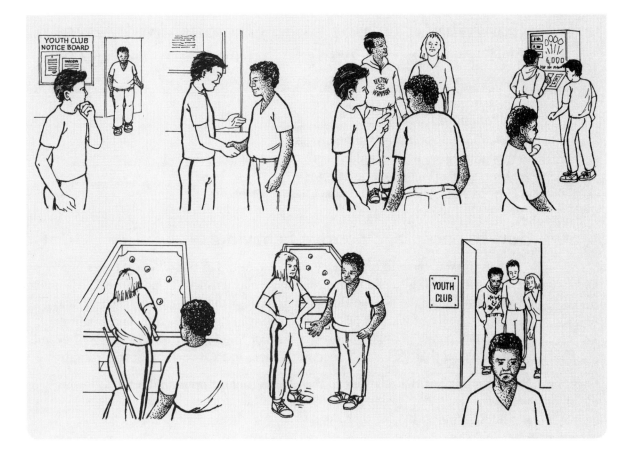

CONSOLIDATION

1 Recall an instance when you have dealt with a new child or young person. You may have introduced them to the setting and people there. Record the details, remembering to include what you did and your rationale (why you did it).

2 During your playwork sessions you will interact with children and young people. Use a diary to record instances when you:

- communicate in a way appropriate to their age and development
- encourage children or young people to ask questions, offer ideas or make suggestions
- encourage children or young people to make choices and control their own play
- actively listen to children
- show respect for individuals
- apply anti-discriminatory practice
- give individual attention to children or young people that is fair to the child and the rest of the group
- respect confidential information.

Remember to describe what you did and give details to enable the reader (your assessor) to gain a clear picture of each instance.

Contribute to positive relationships between children/young people and others in the play setting

What you need to learn
- How to encourage **positive behaviour**.
- Why guidelines and boundaries are important.
- Diversity and emotional development.
- How to manage conflict and challenging behaviour.

How to encourage positive behaviour

As a playworker, you will experience many examples of the different types of behaviour that children and young people display. Positive behaviour is constructive and appropriate to the play setting. It is behaviour that recognises, respects and values others. By promoting positive behaviour in the play setting and treating children and young people as individuals according to their own needs, we become role models for them. This will encourage them to treat each other accordingly.

Encouraging positive behaviour in the play setting is important for the following reasons:
- it helps create a relaxed atmosphere
- it ensures the smooth running of the setting
- it creates a safe environment
- it encourages acceptance of themselves and others
- it helps reinforce the importance of respect
- it helps develop social skills
- it helps develop cooperation.

Examples of positive behaviour are given in the table below.

Types of positive behaviour	Examples
Playing co-operatively	Playing a game, e.g. taking turns with a dice
Playing imaginatively	Dressing up or role-playing situations
Helping others	Helping to carry something, giving out snacks, passing scissors, pens, etc.
Taking care of others	Comforting others when hurt or upset, helping with tasks
Co-operating with the playworker	Completing requests, following instructions, helping others
Contributing to discussions	Giving suggestions, sharing opinions, experimenting
Using appropriate language	Using non-stereotypical language, not discriminating

ACTIVE KNOWLEDGE

To encourage positive behaviour, playworkers need to reflect on the way they think, act and speak, because the best way to promote positive behaviour is by example. Think about how you think, speak and act in your play setting.

1 How do you speak? Do you:
- say please when asking children and young people to do things
- thank them for completing or trying to complete tasks you have set
- use a commanding tone when giving instructions
- shout across the room
- say no, without explanations?

2 How do you act? Do you:
- wait your turn for a sandwich or just take one first
- drink coffee and expect the children to have water or juice
- choose activities you enjoy
- choose not to go outside when it is cold
- gravitate towards children who look and smell nice?

3 What do you think? Do you:
- think a child is spoilt
- think certain children have what you see as bad manners
- make assumptions about a child's life?

By setting an appropriate example of positive behaviour by being non-judgemental, you will find that the children and young people will copy your behaviour and you will gradually:
- build up mutual respect
- create unity
- help children and young people to learn socially acceptable behaviour
- increase their acceptance of others.

Keys to good practice: Encouraging positive behaviour

✓ Award stamps for positive behaviour; a variety of stamps are available, e.g. showing smiley faces or animals with smiles, and these can usually be stamped on to a card, book or hand.

✓ Award stickers for positive behaviour; a range of stickers can be bought or made that praise and encourage children and young people.

✓ Inform parents or carers about positive behaviour.

✓ Award certificates for positive behaviour.

✓ Reward positive behaviour with the opportunity to choose an activity, video, game, etc.

✓ Reward positive behaviour by giving appropriate responsibility, e.g. handing out the food and drink at snack time.

✓ Reward positive behaviour by displaying examples of work.

✓ Reward positive behaviour by telling or showing others.

Whatever method you choose it should be appropriate to the situation and the child or young person. Things that do not cost much are often the most effective rewards. It is important that these are not seen as bribes, as you may find that the rewards become a competitive alternative rather than an effective method of rewarding positive behaviour.

Why guidelines and boundaries are important

Within a play setting, you will need to have guidelines and boundaries (often referred to as **ground rules**). There are many reasons why guidelines are important:

- they raise awareness of safety of self and others
- they aid security
- they comply with legislation
- to create a relaxed atmosphere
- to meet parents' expectations
- to maintain equipment and material
- they are an insurance and inspection requirement.

Most importantly, guidelines help to ensure that play activities can be carried out as safely and securely as possible. They also help playworkers implement the Play Values (see page 1).

Playworkers will have their own ideas about the rules they think are important within a play setting. Each person will base their own rules on their own ideas (values and priorities) and also on their experience in working with children in a play setting. It is important not to try to force your ideas on to others, especially if their values differ from yours. Open-minded discussions are necessary.

When discussing rules it is important to keep in mind the wellbeing and welfare of the children and young people and your aim of providing a happy, welcoming but safe environment. Too many rules can hinder play, and while you want to create a safe and secure environment, children and young people should be encouraged and challenged by stimulating activities and experiences. They should be allowed to experiment and take risks within a safe environment, and to participate in as much free play as possible. This does not mean that they should be allowed to cause damage or harm to people or the setting. They should be guided towards setting and negotiating ground rules for themselves. If children and young people are involved in negotiating guidelines and boundaries, this can help to:

- provide a child centred environment
- encourage children to adhere to the guidelines
- provide a negotiating point when challenging behaviour
- encourage children to become involved in the setting
- encourage children to become aware of health, safety and security issues
- show you value their opinions
- provide a positive experience for the children, to build their self-esteem and self-confidence
- encourage mutual respect.

When ground rules are initially set, it is crucial to involve as many of the children and young people as possible. Using a variety of informal discussions and formal group discussions, for example questionnaires, playworkers can decide on the rules that will be effective in the particular setting.

Keys to good practice: Setting ground rules

✓ Let everyone take part; sit all the children down together and let everyone make suggestions.

✓ Have one person write the suggestions down on a flip chart.

✓ Let everyone voice their opinion and ideas.

✓ Discuss each idea realistically and non-judgementally.

✓ If a suggestion is unrealistic, turn it into a positive suggestion by negotiation and explain your reasons.

✓ Do not use sarcasm or put-downs to suggestions.

✓ Do not force your ideas on the children and young people. They can and will think for themselves.

✓ Give hints about areas of concern if they are unable to think of things themselves.

Once you have a set of rules, you will probably find that they read like the one below:

No fighting	No swearing	No stealing from others	No pushing

These focus on a negative attitude, but when trying to reinforce positive behaviour you can encourage the children or young people to turn these rules around to focus on the positive, for example:

- no fighting – treat others as you would like to be treated yourself, respect other people and their bodies by avoiding physical contact
- no swearing – speak to others in a tone and manner that shows respect
- no stealing – respect other people's possessions.

ACTIVE KNOWLEDGE

Look at your setting's ground rules.

1 Are they written in a positive manner?
2 Find out who wrote them and when they were last reviewed.

The types of rules, and the language level in which they are written, will depend on the age and development level of the children or young people in your setting. An example of a behaviour policy for the Calverton out-of-school club is given on page 22.

In order to reinforce the ground rules in your setting, the following ideas could be implemented.

- Encourage children and young people to use the club name to make a poster or a poem incorporating the rules, for example:

ACE CLUB

A – Always treat others as you would like to be treated yourself.
C – Calling names hurts; speak with respect.
E – Everyone should feel welcome and accepted at the club.

C – Culture and background are important, so respect them.
L – Leave toys and equipment as you would like to find them.
U – Understand that people have personal things that they do not want others to take.
B – By following these rules we will have a happy club.

- When re-enforcing ground rules try to use positive language yourself. You can say no in many forms without using the exact words, for example instead of saying, 'no, don't do that', you could say 'I really would like you to do this instead of that'.

- An interesting experience for staff and children is to have a 'no no day'. This is a day when everyone is not allowed to use the word 'no' (except in emergencies, e.g. to prevent a serious accident like touching a live wire). This creates a calm atmosphere and encourages everyone to think before they speak.

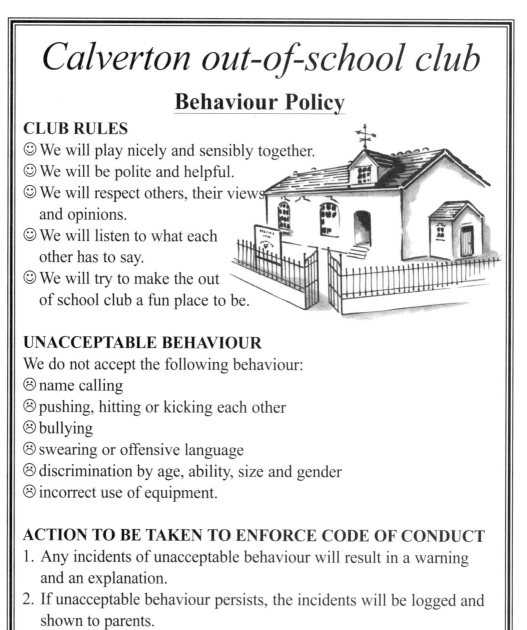

Calverton out-of-school club

Behaviour Policy

CLUB RULES

- ☺ We will play nicely and sensibly together.
- ☺ We will be polite and helpful.
- ☺ We will respect others, their views and opinions.
- ☺ We will listen to what each other has to say.
- ☺ We will try to make the out of school club a fun place to be.

UNACCEPTABLE BEHAVIOUR

We do not accept the following behaviour:

- ☹ name calling
- ☹ pushing, hitting or kicking each other
- ☹ bullying
- ☹ swearing or offensive language
- ☹ discrimination by age, ability, size and gender
- ☹ incorrect use of equipment.

ACTION TO BE TAKEN TO ENFORCE CODE OF CONDUCT

1. Any incidents of unacceptable behaviour will result in a warning and an explanation.
2. If unacceptable behaviour persists, the incidents will be logged and shown to parents.
3. Any incidents of persistent or serious unacceptable behaviour may result in a suspension from the club for a period of time. This will be

Diversity and emotional development

Everyone is unique and has their own opinions and ideas about what is important to them. The children or young people in your setting will come from differing backgrounds and cultures. They will have different values and priorities that arise from their families and friends. As a playworker, you should be non-judgemental and accepting of the differences, and should lead by example. The play setting aim should be to show respectful awareness of all major events in the lives of the children and families in the setting, and in society as a whole. Playworkers should welcome the diversity of backgrounds from which the children, young people and staff come. Children should be encouraged to celebrate a wide range of cultural festivals as part of the diversity of life.

All children should be respected and each child's **individuality** and potential should be recognised, valued and nurtured. Activities and opportunities that are provided, and the use of play equipment, should offer children opportunities to develop in an environment that is free from prejudice and discrimination. Appropriate opportunities should be given to children to explore, acknowledge and value similarities and differences between themselves and others.

Emotional development is an ongoing process for children and young people and will extend into their adult lives. A playworker can play a key role in helping in this development by providing a range of activities and opportunities that enable children and young people to express freely their opinions, ideas and emotions. This should be in a caring and safe environment where children know that the adults are supportive. It is important for children and young people to understand the feelings of other people for the following reasons:

- so they can offer support to others
- so they understand why others are happy or upset
- so they can react appropriately
- so they can sympathise.

A playworker can support and encourage children and young people in their emotional development by explaining why people are behaving as they are, and by helping them to understand and deal with their emotions appropriately.

How to manage conflict and challenging behaviour

There will be many occasions when a playworker will observe challenging and unwanted behaviour. Each setting will have a behaviour policy that is accessible to staff and parents or carers. The action you take to address conflict and challenging behaviour should follow the guidelines set out in the National Standards.

Standard X: Challenging and unwanted behaviour

A playworker must understand what challenging and unwanted behaviour is; that is, actions that are unsafe or any behaviour that may cause harm or damage (physical, verbal or emotional) to the child, young person or others in the setting, or to the setting, for example fighting, bullying, racist comments, physical threats, material damage.

Challenging behaviour could affect the child or young person's play experiences and opportunities as shown in the diagram below.

Staff time is taken up dealing with the unwanted behaviour.

Unwanted behaviour needs constant attention, which will inhibit the child's play

Other children may reject and not want to play with the child.

The play environment becomes unsafe.

The child will miss out on activities and opportunities.

Challenging behaviour affects everyone in the setting

If the unwanted behaviour involves children using equipment dangerously, this could cause an injury. If a playworker is able to intervene before situations become volatile, the behaviour can often be diverted or stopped. A sensitive approach in these situations can be an advantage for both children and young people involved and others in the vicinity. Once a child or young person becomes angry, they can lose their common sense and reasoning; it is then that they can become a danger to themselves and others. By building a good relationship with children and young people in the care setting, you will become aware of trigger situations and the techniques to use for the de-escalation of such situations. A consistent approach by the staff team will help workers to cope and feel supported.

Keys to good practice: Strategies for dealing with the early stages of unwanted behaviour

✓ Ignore it as long as the child or others are in no danger.
✓ Distract the child; try to divert their attention to calmer topics.
✓ Praise positive aspects of behaviour; this often surprises the child as he or she will not be expecting this response.
✓ Remind the child about the code of behaviour, especially if he or she helped to set it up.
✓ Discuss and negotiate situations and issues.
✓ Monitor the child to see if he or she can sort things out without help.
✓ Use appropriate humour.

Keys to good practice: Techniques once behaviour becomes more serious

✓ Try to calm the child down.
✓ Give them space and time.
✓ Stay calm yourself, be firm but reassuring.
✓ Be careful what you say; do not make threats that are unrealistic or personal.
✓ Move any children who may be watching into another area.

Once a calm atmosphere has been restored, it may be possible to discuss with the child the reasons for the behaviour and work towards a behaviour modification programme. It may be useful to involve the parents or carers, asking them to continue a consistent approach at home.

If you monitor and record child behaviour, this will enable you to make referrals or enlist extra support services. It will also help with long term strategies, as you will have a document to work with and from. Your setting may have a set form for recording incidents (an incident sheet), like the one on page 26.

challenge others when situations arise. Children should be supported in trying to deal with the conflict themselves, and a playworker can help this process by:

- not reacting instantly and taking full control (unless it is a dangerous situation)
- acting as a facilitator or a mediator for both sides, offering options for an amicable solution
- supporting the children by confirming legal or setting procedures.

ACTIVE KNOWLEDGE

1 Look at the diagrams below and say when you would have intervened and why.

2 For each of the following examples, what you would do and why? Remember to state how you would deal with the victim.

- At your setting, you are sitting near a group of children when you overhear one 8-year-old girl telling a 6-year-old Afro-Caribbean boy, 'You can't play with me because your skin is dirty brown'.
- A group of children are teasing a child who has two mums and no dad.
- After dividing the children into two teams for a game of football, one team start complaining loudly that it is unfair because they have the child with a calliper on his leg.

Element PW1.3 | # Contribute to positive relationships with parents and carers

What you need to learn
- Why it is important to value parents and carers.
- How to maintain good relationships with parents and carers.
- Ways of communicating with parents and carers.
- How to deal with misunderstandings and complaints.

Why it is important to value parents and carers

A playworker's role includes establishing and maintaining relationships with parents and carers. This is so you can work in partnership with them in caring for their children. You will both have the same ultimate target – the wellbeing of their child/children.

When we use the term parent in this book we refer to the main carer of a child or young person. This could be his or her mother, father, grandparent, aunt, uncle, foster parent or legal guardian. Parents are children's first carers. From their parents, children will acquire their name, their place within the family and their social background. From their social background, their culture and religion emerge. Children's early experiences impact on their personality. Parents are usually the child's first educators.

It is important to remember that parents have the key role in the upbringing of their child. They have, after all, known the child for a long time! They have a special bond that is unique, and which another adult cannot replace. The role of the playworker is to support the parent in their parenting role by showing respect for his or her position, and by working in partnership with the parent to achieve what is best for the child or young person. The ultimate responsibility in all aspects of child care lies with the parent.

The main aim of the Children Act (1989) was to form a balance (similar to a seesaw). On one side is the child and his or her needs and rights, and on the other side are the parents and their rights and responsibilities. By forming a balance between the two, the wellbeing of the child will be protected. The National

Standards provide guidelines about working in partnership with parents and carers, as shown below.

Standard 12: Working in partnership with parents and carers

- The registered person and staff work in partnership with parents to meet the needs of the children, both individually and as a group. Information is given to parents which includes:
  - basic written information about the setting, e.g. the admissions policy, hours, contact information, staffing, routines, etc.
  - written complaints procedures which include the address and telephone number of the regulator
  - information about activities provided for children
  - details of policies and procedures.
- Volunteers or committee members are given full information and guidance on their roles and responsibilities.
- There is a system in place for the exchange of information between parents and staff members. Appropriate and prompt action is taken on any concerns raised and a record of all complaints is maintained.
- Staff are aware of the need to maintain privacy and confidentiality.
- Parents have access to all written records about their children.
- Arrangements are made with parents about the arrival and departure of children to and from the provision, including making sure that the right person collects children. Children are only released from the provision to individuals named by the parents.
- If a child is identified as a child in need, the registered person, usually with parental permission, gives appropriate information to referring agencies.

How to maintain good relationships with parents and carers

Playworkers should build and maintain relationships with parents for the following reasons:

- to develop trust
- to ensure good lines of communication
- to encourage participation in the setting and make them feel welcome and valued
- to set a good example (role model) for the children and young people
- to build a good reputation; this could lead to parents recommending your setting to other parents
- to boost the self-esteem and confidence of parents
- because you may need the co-operation or help of the parents from time to time
- to find out and meet the children's needs
- to enhance your understanding of the child
- to provide stability and consistency for the child
- to make yourself more approachable if the parents have a problem.

There are many ways you, as a playworker, can help to make a parent feel welcome when they come to your setting for the first time, as shown in the diagram below.

Welcoming parents to your setting

First impressions count, and if you want parents to use your facility they need to feel comfortable with you and the other workers, as well as the setting.

CASE STUDY

Your supervisor has invited Zak's mother to look around the club. You meet her at the door and begin to introduce her to the setting.

1 What would you say to her when you first meet?
2 How would you find out about her expectations and requirements of the setting?

Ways of communicating with parents and carers

It is important to maintain relationships with parents; you could do this by offering opportunities for them to become involved in the play setting, for example:

- you could ask parents to join the management committee or other group
- you could involve parents in fund raising, visits and outings
- you could invite parents to social events
- you could enlist their help with specialist skills, e.g. woodwork.

The effect discrimination can have on parents

Parents come from a variety of social backgrounds and, as a playworker, you should respect their individuality, and social and cultural background. Some parents may have had a strict upbringing while others will have had a much more relaxed upbringing. A non-judgemental attitude should always be adopted, with an open mind to the values and priorities of others. Your concern is the wellbeing of the child. All that matters is that the child is happy, loved and cared for. To respect individuality is to accept others; this will enhance the relationship you have with parents.

Parents' wishes regarding their children, for example dietary needs or hygiene customs, should be allowed whenever possible, as long as the wishes meet the policies and procedures of the setting. Sometimes the wishes of the parent may conflict with the ground rules or policies of the setting. Your first concern is for the wellbeing of the child or young person. In all instances you should be honest and state your reasons if you are unable to comply with the parent's wishes. It may be that you can back this decision with legislation, and the setting's **agreed policies and procedures**. If the parent is still not happy, then you should refer them to your senior playworker or line manager.

✓ ACTIVE KNOWLEDGE

1 Think about what would you do and why in the following situations.

- A parent asks you to smack her 6-year-old daughter if she wets her pants.
- A parent sends her 11-year-old son to collect his sister aged 5 from your play setting.
- A parent asks you not to let her son paint or do any other creative activity where he may get his hands dirty.
- A parent asks you which child had head lice last week and not to let her child near that person.

Part of a playworker's job description will probably include a section about interactions with parents, as shown below.

Have good interpersonal and communication skills with peers, children and their parents or carers, with regard to confidentiality at all times.

When communicating with parents and carers it is important to choose methods to suit individual circumstances. If parents have basic literacy problems or cannot read well in English, face-to-face communication and provision of information in other languages may be needed.

How to deal with misunderstandings and complaints

There are times within any work setting when misunderstandings occur. In play settings these misunderstandings could be between:

- children and young people
- workers
- management
- parents.

A misunderstanding is a matter that may have been misinterpreted, for example a parent may have thought that the play scheme provided a free meal when in fact it is necessary for the parent to pay for it. Misunderstandings can soon escalate and become serious issues or problems. As a setting, you should have a policy, either in writing or at least an agreed policy, that if a misunderstanding occurs it is dealt with as soon as possible and in the most appropriate manner.

When a misunderstanding arises, you should ask yourself, 'Can I deal with this myself, do I need advice or assistance?' If you feel you can deal with the problem yourself, and it is a minor misunderstanding that can easily be put right, then address the issue sensitively yourself. If there is an element of doubt then seek advice; this could be from a senior playworker or your line manager. Weigh up and discuss the options and the possible outcomes, bearing in mind that the welfare of the child is the main focus.

If the misunderstanding is of a more serious nature, then you need to follow the polices and procedures of your setting. Much will depend upon the type of misunderstanding or complaint. You should complete a report on the incident, ensuring that you sign and date it. You may need a witness if the matter is of a more serious nature. Remember that your setting will have a complaints procedure; the parent should have a copy of this or should be directed to its location within the setting. Always remain calm and controlled, and adopt a sensitive but professional manner. State your case and back it up with reasons. Refer to the policies and procedures of the setting. An example of a complaints procedure is given on page 33.

Complaints procedure for Homestead out-of-school club

Making complaints known

A parent who is uneasy about any of the out of school club's policies should first talk over any worries with the officer in charge. If this does not have a satisfactory outcome or if the problem occurs again, the parent should put the concerns or the complaint in writing and request a meeting with the officer in charge. Both the parent and the officer in charge should have a friend or partner present if required, and an agreed written record of the discussion should be made, a copy of which should be made available to both parties.

Most complaints should be resolved informally at this initial stage

If the matter is still not settled to the parent's satisfaction, the parent should again contact the officer in charge. If no agreement can be reached, it might be helpful to request the services of an external mediator. A mediator has no legal powers but may help clarify the situation. Staff within the out of school club will be available to act as mediators if both parties request it. The mediator will help define the problem, review the action taken so far and suggest further ways in which it might be resolved. The mediator will keep all discussions confidential, will meet with the out of school club if requested, and will keep a written record of all meetings that are held. Copies of these will be given to all parties concerned.

The role of the registering authority

In some cases, it will be necessary to bring in OfSTED who have a duty to ensure that specified requirements are adhered to, and with whom the out of school club works in partnership to encourage high standards. The registering authority will become involved if a child appears to be at risk, or where there is a possible breach of registration requirements. In these cases, both the parents and the out of school club would be informed, and the officer in charge would work with OfSTED to ensure that a proper investigation of the complaint is followed by appropriate action.

ACTIVE KNOWLEDGE

1 Read your setting's complaints policy to identify the procedure you should follow in dealing with misunderstandings and complaints. Find out where your complaints procedures are located.

2 Think about what you would say and what would you do in the following circumstances.

- A parent complains that the club has overcharged her for the weekly sessions.
- An irate father comes into the setting demanding that you tell him who caused the mark on his son's leg during a game of football.

CASE STUDY

Mr Taylor comes in and is quite angry. He says that his daughter, Kia, who is 4 years old, came home in tears last night after attending the club. Kia said she was upset because she did not get a drink of orange when the other children did. Mr Taylor is very cross as he claims that, 'this is not the first time his daughter has missed out'.

1 What would you say and do in this situation?
2 How would you ensure that Kia was involved in activities in the future?

CONSOLIDATION

1 Use a diary to record the time when you first met a parent, and how you continued to develop the relationship with them over a period of time.

2 Recall a time when you have acted on the wishes of a parent with regard to the care of his or her child. Evaluate your actions and relate them to your setting's polices and procedures.

3 If you have ever had a misunderstanding with a parent or a complaint that you then passed on, write about this situation. Remember to observe confidentiality.

END OF UNIT TEST

1 What would you say to a child at a first meeting?

2 How would you encourage children and young people to become involved in the opportunities and activities available in your setting?

3 List three ways of involving children in developing ground rules.

4 Give examples of how you would reward positive behaviour.

5 Give two examples of why it is important to value parents and carers.

6 How could you encourage parents and carers to become involved in the setting?

Support children and young people's play

Play should be stimulating and an enjoyable experience for children and young people. It should contain opportunities for them to take risks, explore challenges and express themselves. Play is a valuable developmental learning tool through which children and young people explore their environment and their feelings, and practise and improve their skills.

This unit is divided into four elements:

- PW2.1 Create a range of environments for children and young people's play.
- PW2.2 Offer a range of play opportunities to children and young people.
- PW2.3 Support children and young people's rights and choices in play.
- PW2.4 End play sessions.

The Play Values covered in this unit are shown below:

Value No	Statement
1	The child must be at the centre of the process.
3	Play should be freely chosen and directed by the child or young person within the guidelines of the setting.
4	An environment must be provided that stimulates and provides opportunities for risks and challenges, and growth of confidence and self-esteem.
6	Every child is an individual and should be respected for who they are.
8	As playworker, you should promote equal opportunities for all children and young people in your setting, regardless of ability, race, culture, social background, etc.
9	Within a play setting, you should be a positive role model and create co-operative working.
12	The play environment should be accessible to all.

Play is an important part of a child's life. By playing a child will:

- develop
- learn
- practise skills
- experiment
- explore
- experience emotions.

Allow children to freely choose their own play opportunities

Children and young people need to play, and your role as a playworker is to provide for play. It is vital that the opportunities you provide for play are freely chosen by the children and young people, and that the play has the potential to let the children develop it spontaneously. It is not necessary for adults to be involved in the play. You should supervise and ensure safety without actually joining in or interfering. The National Standards state the following about play:

Play values 1 and 2

- Children's play is freely chosen, personally directed behaviour, motivated from within; through play, the child explores the world and his/her relationship with it, elaborating all the while a flexible range of responses to the challenges he/she encounters; by playing, the child learns and develops as an individual.
- Whereas children may play without encouragement or help, adults can, through the provision of an appropriate human and physical environment, significantly enhance opportunities for the child to play creatively and thus develop through play.

These assumptions underpin all playwork practice; they give guidance and explanations with regard to good practice. By reading and following the National Standards, the setting will provide for play in a way that advantages the children or young people, and this will help them to develop and play in a way that gives them choice and personal direction.

The child should always be at the centre of any play activity; this means that the play opportunities should focus on the children, on what they want and need. How a child or young person plays can be classified into four categories:

- **observation** – a child will copy an action demonstrated to them, e.g. hitting a ball with a racquet
- **exploration** – encouraging the child to try a new activity, e.g. go-karting or tag games where children will be learning new skills and socialising
- **experimentation** – providing time and space for the child to have a go at an activity in a relaxed environment
- **repetitiveness** – to gain more of an understanding of a particular activity or skill, children will want to repeat it.

Another way children and young people gather information is by using their five senses: sight, smell, taste, touch and hearing. For example, if the children ask for an activity about food and you provide a food tasting opportunity, it would involve using the senses as shown in the table below.

Sense	Example of information
Sight	Comparing fruit from different countries, and of different colours, shapes, sizes.
Hearing	Learning about the produce, where it comes from and how it grows.
Taste	Tasting the produce (bitter, sweet, sour).
Touch	Feeling the texture (hard, soft, prickly).
Smell	Scent of the produce (pleasant, unpleasant).

Playworkers need to provide sufficient opportunities, resources and activities to encourage children to use their senses to gain experiences and knowledge they can use in later life.

While children and young people are playing, they may from time to time make mistakes. This is not a failure but part of a learning curve. By making mistakes, a child or young person will learn from them and be able to redirect their aim.

Developmental experiences are also present in play opportunities – children develop through play. The range of development experiences to be offered within the play environment can be remembered by the acronym **SPICE:**

S social interaction

P physical activity

I intellectual stimulation

C creative achievement

E emotional stability

Social interaction – this involves any kind of interaction, for example when the child or young person:

- takes turns
- relates to relatives and friends
- co-operates with others
- shares
- leads or works as part of a team
- relates to other adults or children.

Physical activity – this includes fine and gross motor skills, for example when the child or young person:

- uses hand/eye coordination
- practises or learns new skills
- uses fine finger control
- uses balancing skills
- uses whole body co-ordination
- uses and controls muscles.

Intellectual stimulation – this is gaining or improving knowledge, for example when the child or young person:

- experiments
- uses imagination
- thinks carefully
- solves problems
- is creative
- uses memory
- experiences concepts
- uses and learns terminology.

Creative achievement – this involves anything that a child or young person creates using their imagination, for example when the child or young person:

- uses practical/theoretical skills
- creates an object or image
- produces something
- uses imagination or initiative.

Emotional stability – this involves personal feelings, for example when the child or young person is:

- confident
- loving
- thrilled
- distressed
- happy
- relaxed
- resentful
- confused
- angry
- pleased
- amused
- cross
- proud
- sad
- wary.

Developmental areas of play are sometimes described differently or include more categories such as:

- **social and moral** – including acceptable behaviour within society, consideration for others, behaving responsibly
- **aesthetic and spiritual** – including beauty, inspiring creativity, life and cultural experiences, acceptance and belonging
- **sensory** – relating to the five senses
- **languages** – development of vocabulary and understanding of terminology.

One play activity can meet many developmental categories, for example the developmental value of outdoor physical play is shown in the diagram below.

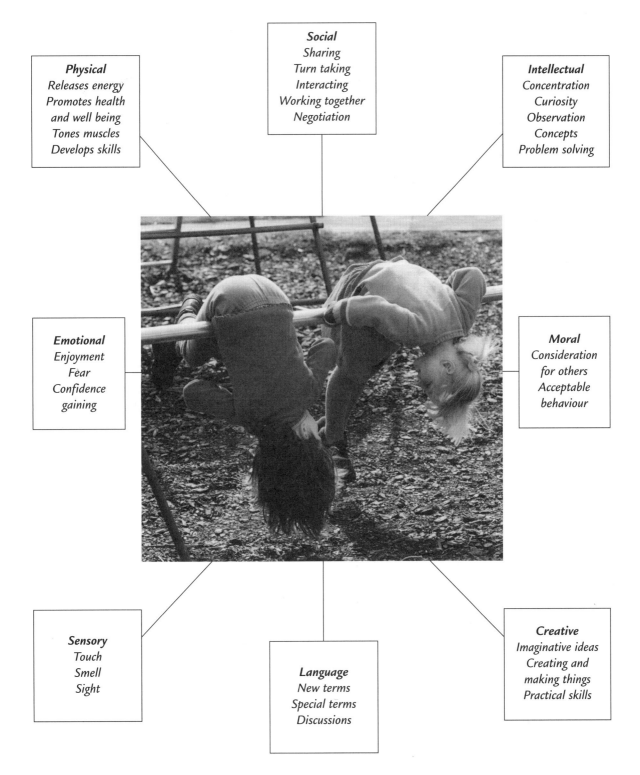

Social
Sharing
Turn taking
Interacting
Working together
Negotiation

Physical
Releases energy
Promotes health
and well being
Tones muscles
Develops skills

Intellectual
Concentration
Curiosity
Observation
Concepts
Problem solving

Emotional
Enjoyment
Fear
Confidence
gaining

Moral
Consideration
for others
Acceptable
behaviour

Sensory
Touch
Smell
Sight

Language
New terms
Special terms
Discussions

Creative
Imaginative ideas
Creating and
making things
Practical skills

Outdoor physical play meets many development categories

There are many different types of play. Below are examples which playworkers need to provide for.

- **Physical play** – this is play that involves physical activity; it can include play that exercises muscles, develops eye and hand co-ordination, develops fine and gross motor skills, etc.
- **Environmental play** – this is play that takes place in the environment, in cities as well as rural areas. It can be indoors or outdoors; it raises awareness to or involves natural elements. It can lead on to craftwork, artwork or drama.
- **Creative play** – this is when children and young people use their imagination to create, invent or produce things. Creative play is an important way to encourage children to experiment and explore the world around them. They discover things by using their senses.
- **Cultural play** – this is how play can value, celebrate and raise awareness of different cultures. Play can enhance learning, understanding and acceptance.
- **Imaginative play** – this is where children and young people use their imagination, where they 'pretend' or act out situations of fantasy. It is sometimes called role-play. It allows children and young people to explore a variety of different situations. Sometimes the roles are portrayed through other objects, e.g. puppets.

A playworker should understand and be aware that children and young people can and will want to play without adult involvement, and by providing a safe physical environment, children will play more creatively and develop through play. Supervision levels and ratios within the setting should meet the inspection requirements. This will help to ensure the safety and security of the children and young people in your care. A playworker should understand the different levels of supervision and use their own initiative and intuition to judge if their involvement in play will enhance or inhibit. This approach will help the play to be self-directed. Play should be self-directed for the following reasons:

- to help give children independence
- to help children learn through play
- to give freedom of choice
- to encourage decision making
- to help children excel in their own achievements
- to boost self-esteem
- to lead to all round development
- to help build confidence
- to encourage discovery and exploration
- to help children interpret meaning
- to help children learn about the consequences of their decisions.

Whatever play opportunities are available, they should focus on the children and young people's interests and needs. Play opportunities should be developmentally appropriate, stimulating and appealing. All children are very different. Their needs can be very simple or very complex and will constantly be changing and developing. The play opportunities you offer should be geared towards meeting these needs – especially any **additional** or **particular needs** a child may have. To identify these needs, you should have a knowledge of the individual children or young people in your setting, plus knowledge of child development. If the setting does not meet the needs of the children and young people attending, then the children will become bored and it is highly likely that attendances will fall.

Create a range of environments for children and young people's play

What you need to learn

- Why the setting should meet the children and young people's needs.
- How to identify children's play needs.
- How to ensure play is stimulating.
- Guidelines that you should follow.

Why the setting should meet the children and young people's needs

Children and young people will have differing interests and needs. It is therefore important that the play setting reflects this by providing a variety of environments that will enhance development. A setting should provide a range of opportunities that cover all the different play areas, and which meet the development needs of the different children and young people who attend. The term used for this is 'child centred'.

When creating a play environment, it is advisable to ask the children or young people in your setting what they would like. If you do not ask those in your care and set out activities you think that they would like, you will be disappointed at the lack of interest a child or young person may show. Also, if your setting does not appear stimulating or challenging to a child or young person they will be reluctant to attend. This could be in relation to the physical environment, from the decoration and the layout to the equipment and materials that you provide. The setting therefore needs to be child centred. Asking the children and young people what they want will help them to feel that the environment is their own.

There are many benefits to the children and young people, the staff and the parents of a child centred setting. Some examples of why the setting should be child centred are shown on page 42.

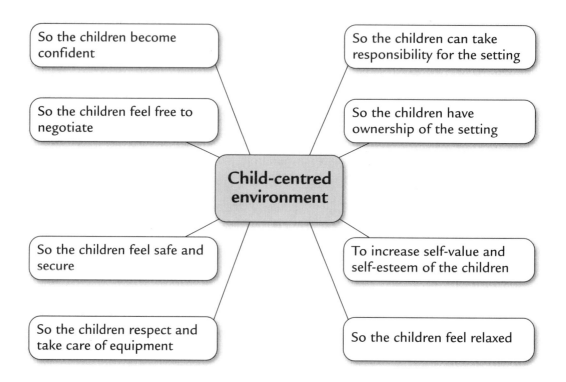

Playworkers can help in this process by helping to make the environment friendly, attractive, stimulating and challenging, as shown in the table below.

Friendly	Look and be enthusiastic; show an interest in the children; use a range of techniques to welcome children and young people and create a welcoming atmosphere; invite children to do things and ask for things.
Attractive	Use screens to display pictures or interesting posters that will encourage creativity.
Stimulating and challenging	Have activities where children can succeed but that include a challenge; recognise effort and achievement; use praise and encouragement; review and develop decor and layout; change things around frequently.

How to identify children's play needs

The play needs of the children and young people in your setting can be identified:

- through the use of trained staff who have sound knowledge of the children's needs
- by giving children choices
- by using effective listening and communication skills
- by asking the children for input, and valuing and implementing their ideas.

To ensure that the environment is meeting the needs of the children and young people that attend, feedback from them will enable you to assess and improve the service you provide. To monitor children or young people's involvement in a setting you can use the following techniques.

- **Observation** – do the children or young people look bored or only half interested in the activity?

- **Questionnaires** – some settings distribute questionnaires to ascertain which activities the children enjoyed.
- **Monitoring forms** – these are similar to questionnaires; staff complete them with the children each evening to monitor the success of the play opportunity.
- **Suggestion box** – this is emptied weekly, and is another way children and young people can contribute to the weekly planning of activities.
- **Children forums** – where staff and children can discuss future events, needs and equipment, etc.
- **Chats** – everyday you will talk to the children; by asking them, 'Did you enjoy that activity? Would you do it again?', you can encourage them to freely provide you with feedback.

ACTIVE KNOWLEDGE

1 Think of a time when you received feedback. Which method did you use?

2 Design a questionnaire to give out at your setting about what play the children and young people would like.

CASE STUDY

While a group of children aged 9–11 in your club are having a snack, they begin to discuss their plans for the summer holidays.

1 How would you use this opportunity to improve and plan for the club's summer activities?

How to ensure play is stimulating

Examples of the types of environments within a play setting that can stimulate children and young people's play are given in the table below.

Environment	Materials and equipment
Craft area	Paint, malleable materials, crayons and boxes
Role play area	Dressing up clothes, cooking utensils, pretend food
Quiet area	Books, tapes, soft cushions, bean bags
Soft play area	Large soft shapes, balls
Computer corner	Computer/video games, play station
Construction area	Lego, small- and large-scale construction toys
Music area	Musical instruments, radios, tapes, TV, video, Karaoke machine, dance mats
Physical area (indoors/outdoors)	Bats, balls, bicycles, skipping ropes, pool table, football table
Games	Board games, fantasy games, quiz games
Food area	Cooking equipment, utensils, chairs, tables, snacks and drinks

Playworkers can help by providing resources, materials and equipment; however, the more involvement the children and young people have, the more child centred the setting becomes.

✓ ACTIVE KNOWLEDGE

Plan an activity or discussion about what the children and young people in your setting would do if you won the lottery and had unlimited funds to spend on the setting. You could provide catalogues and magazines to help them decide, and you could encourage the children and young people to think of ways to present their ideas.

To ensure the play environment is stimulating, you need to be aware of the following as a playworker:

- **Age range** – in a play setting the age range can be vast; through experience you will learn to adapt activities to meet the different ages and developmental levels.
- **Abilities** – if the equipment and materials promote activities that are too easy, the children will become bored; if they are too difficult, they may become frustrated or lose interest in the activity. Find the level that is appropriate.
- **Interests** – by knowing the children you will have a better understanding of the type of opportunities and activities they like to participate in, and you can then make these available.
- **Staff supervision** – different activities require various levels of supervision; this may mean that you need to have a rota or a programme to include everyone's requests.
- **Resources** – make sure you have sufficient equipment for all to participate and that equipment is in good working order.
- **Play space** – check that your floor space can house activities safely; again, you may need a floor rota to create opportunities for all.
- **Number of participants** – too many children and insufficient resources increase the risk of danger. Children and young people can take turns as long as they are informed beforehand.
- **Sufficient time** – there is no point starting a long activity 15 minutes before the end of a session. Participants will feel frustrated that they cannot complete the task.

If all of the above are taken into consideration then a **play opportunity** should be fun and run smoothly, and children or young people will feel they have both enjoyed it and learned something from it.

CASE STUDY

Tom is 12 years old and enjoys environmental play outside, in particular he enjoys building. However today it has rained constantly. Finally, he comes over to you and says, 'I'm bored!'

1 What would be your reply?
2 How could you use this situation to help Tom find play opportunities of interest?

Guidelines that you should follow

Guidelines are set out to help playworkers focus on the play opportunities that they should provide and to ensure that the setting is safe, hygienic and secure. You will find guidelines in your setting of the **organisation's policies and procedures** and these will relate to the National Standards.

A job description for a playworker will usually involve points that focus on the working environment, for example:

> Help provide a safe and welcoming child-centred environment which meets the needs of all the children attending.

A job description sets out the basis for your expected performance and duties, and once you sign your contract it will be a legal document.

The Play Values also include sections about the environment, for example Play Value 4 states:

> Every child has a right to a play environment which stimulates and provides opportunities for risks and challenges and the growth of confidence and self-esteem.

These guidelines help playworkers to determine the type of environment that is needed. Each setting will have its own aims and objectives and these also will include aspects relating to the environment. You may find that your setting's aims are similar to the ones below.

> The overall aims of the Calverton out-of-school club are to:
> - recruit and monitor high quality staff who meet the needs of all children
> - encourage progress by providing a safe, nurturing and stimulating environment
> - generate a happy environment with warm and caring staff.

Your setting's policies and procedures should meet the National Standards, as shown below:

Standard 4: Safe settings
- The premises should be safe, secure and suitable for their purpose. They provide adequate space in an appropriate location, are welcoming to children and offer access to the necessary facilities for a range of activities which promote their development
- The space standards provide minimum space requirements for the whole provision. The registered person shows how this space will be divided up and used to provide activities for children and how staff will be deployed within it.
- Provision is made (space or partitioned area) for children who wish to relax or play quietly, equipped with appropriate furniture. This area may be converted from normal play space, provided children can rest safely without disturbance.
- Play areas are large enough to give scope for free movement and well spread out activities. There are separate areas for different activities.

The implementation of these guidelines will be checked at inspection and any that are not adhered to will form part of the setting's action plan.

You may find that your playwork team has set practices that it follows with regard to the environment. These may not be legal obligations, or even set in the guidelines, but may well be instances of good playwork practice, for example reviewing and updating the environment on a regular basis. This is important in order to ensure that the environment meets the children's changing needs, and it also helps with:

- keeping the environment challenging, stimulating and interesting
- meeting the developmental changes of the children
- keeping the environment welcoming in appearance, safe and hygienic
- relieving boredom and lack of interest
- updating the environment to meet current interests and developments.

When reviewing the environment, it is good practice to involve a variety of people, such as those shown in the table below.

People involved	Why
Children	It is their facility; they should feel it is a child-centred environment.
Staff	To gain ideas, to enlist help, to enhance team work.
Parents/family	To gain ideas and opinions, to enlist help, to enhance participation.
Other facility users	To ensure the facility is still appropriate to their needs.

ACTIVE KNOWLEDGE

At a staff meeting you are asked to prepare a cultural play environment; you are allocated a display board and a corner of the setting. Discuss the following:

- what you would do
- why you would do it
- the resources you would need
- how you would organise it.

CONSOLIDATION

Recall a time when you created a themed play area within your setting as a result of suggestions and ideas from the children or young people.

If you have not experienced this, try to encourage the children or young people to think of an idea (or theme) that you can help them implement.

Offer a range of play opportunities to children and young people

What you need to learn

- Preparing and planning play opportunities.
- Offering opportunities that can be freely chosen, explored and adapted by children and young people to meet their needs.
- Setting ground rules with and for children and young people.

Preparing and planning play opportunities

Your responsibility as a playworker is to facilitate play. Some play settings have a programme of opportunities and activities and this can be a useful tool for creating opportunities for children to develop and adapt their play. Providing a programme enables settings to plan in advance, and the programme can be made available to children and their parents or carers so they know what is happening.

Despite this, some of the most effective play settings operate without a programme – a lot will depend upon the type of setting in which you work, the age of the children and young people that attend your setting, the expectations of the parents and carers (especially if they pay for the care that you provide) and the settings management ethos.

Programmes can have the following benefits for staff and children:

- they help staff to work together and know what is required
- they help ensure that equipment and materials are available
- they help with planning any visits or celebrations for special occasions
- they ensure staffing levels meet requirements
- they help children and young people feel more secure
- they help ensure children and young people attend in appropriate dress and footwear
- they help to motivate children and young people
- children and young people can see when their ideas are put on the programme.

Programmes also help to meet parental expectations; parents often have more confidence in the play setting if the setting seems well organised. However, if a programme is strict and rigid this will hinder play; children do not need to spend too much time on structured activities, which they do all day at school. Flexibility within the play programme is therefore vital.

If you are to offer a play opportunity or an activity, it is useful to plan so that you are prepared and the equipment and materials are ready for the session. Before the activity, discuss your ideas with your supervisor to ensure that it is a suitable activity for the children and young people in your setting. You can follow set activity plans or use a less formal model. Whatever method you choose make sure that you cover all the possible eventualities and planning guidelines. Some tips and hints are set out below to help you.

- **Beforehand** – ask the children and young people to think of some ideas and then complete the activity plan.
- **The activity** – write what you are going to do. Remember, an activity can be any interaction between you and one or more children, or between children. It does not have to have an end product.
- **Aim** – state what you and the children or young people hope to achieve from the activity and why you have decided to do it.
- **Playworker input** – this section is for you to highlight any specific role you will have, either practically or to promote development, e.g. new vocabulary to be introduced.
- **Health and safety** – highlight any considerations you and the children need to make with regard to both resources and the environment, including a list of who you should notify.
- **Development value** – write what skills and knowledge the children will learn, linking to SPICE (see page 37). Your supervisor may have some helpful suggestions.
- **Resources** – state clearly all the resources you will need and use this as a checklist when you set up the activity.
- **Plan of activity** – use this section to make notes on your activity. These can include diagrams if applicable and instruction points.
- **Implementing the activity** – remember, it is your activity; get involved without stifling the play. Interact and supervise the children as appropriate. Think about the presentation when setting up the activity; if it looks appealing the children are more likely to take part. Make it enjoyable for both the children and yourself. Remember to encourage them to adapt and change things.
- **Evaluation** – write up how it went. Be honest; say if it was a huge success or a terrible disaster. Describe how the children reacted. What surprised you? Did the children gain what you thought they would (look back at your aim and development value) or did the activity promote areas you had not considered? Would you do anything different next time? Did the children deviate from your plan?

At first, planning and doing the activities may not be easy, and recording may be a chore. It will get easier and quicker as you develop, enabling you to link theory to practice and to add value to the input you give to the children or young people. Your setting may have its own activity guidelines or you could use a similar format to the one on page 49.

PLAY ACTIVITY PLAN

Activity title: Bubble making

Play opportunity: Environmental/physical/outdoor play

Aim: To provide a variety of resources that can be used to make bubbles; to encourage the young people to use and develop these different bubbles.

Location: Outside play area

Number of children/young people: 1–20

Age range: 5–15 years

Number of staff: 1–2 depending on number of participating children

Playworker input: To provide bubble liquid and resources, to encourage imagination and adaptation, to introduce scientific and special vocabulary, to aid participation and give encouragement.

Health and safety: Large open space: ensure it is rubbish free, check materials for sharp edges, etc. Highlight the dangers to children/young people regarding:

- bubble liquid in eyes
- slipping on spilt liquid
- bubble liquid in mouth.

Development value:

Social – sharing, taking turns, discussing, helping each other, working together.
Physical – dexterity, fine and gross motor skills, exercising lungs, blowing.
Intellectual – problem solving, how to get bigger bubbles, using terminology relating to scientific concepts.
Creative – making shapes to dip in liquid, finding other materials to use.
Emotional – experiences, success and failure, dealing with emotions.

Resources: Bubble liquid in large bowls, bubble pipes, rings, wire, small hoops, curtain wire, plastic six pack holders, coat hangers, pliers, water aprons for younger children.

Plan: Try it out prior to the activity, get equipment out and readily available, enlist the help of the children to make/decant the liquid into the bowls, explain the health and safety issues, encourage children/young people to take part and experiment, top up materials, help as required, collect more resources if requested.

After the activity, it will help if you evaluate. This will enable you to highlight positive and negative aspects and improve the activity if it is repeated. It may also be useful to discuss the activity with the children and your **colleagues** and ask them for feedback. Most play settings have a file of activity plans as a central resource, so if the activity is repeated by another worker they will be aware of any aspects to repeat or exclude.

Even though you have planned an activity, the children or young people may adapt the resources and completely change it from your plan. This is fine; your role is to provide resources and opportunities which children and young people are free to choose (or not) and adapt as they wish.

Offering opportunities that can be freely chosen, explored and adapted by children and young people to meet their needs

An organised play setting helps children and young people feel secure. To meet inspection requirements and parental expectations, a programme of opportunities and activities is usually available. However, within this programme, when planning opportunities playworkers need to ensure that these are flexible and easily adapted by the children and young people. For example a playworker may provide craft equipment for kite making but the children may decide to develop and adapt the activity to create other things that are seen in the sky, e.g. hot air balloons and aeroplanes, or they may change it into a Chinese theme and make a dragon.

Free and spontaneous play is important and should be in every session. Some people think that structure and play do not go together, but by giving children and young people opportunities to choose and adapt within a flexible programme, play can be enhanced and children can be motivated to create stimulating opportunities. Some sessions on the programme may be left blank to indicate total free play.

Spontaneous play can motivate children to create stimulating opportunities

Programmes, as well as activities and opportunities, should be flexible and, although some framework is required, free choice and free play should be promoted and encouraged.

The example of the kite making activity could progress throughout the afternoon and be further developed by the children and young people. Once an idea is suggested, you as the playworker can build on this and explore different options and opportunities relating to the idea. It is of vital importance that you involve children when planning opportunities. You should discuss your ideas (taken from the children and young people's suggestions) with colleagues and parents or carers. They can contribute in several ways and this will help:

● to ensure co-operation from everyone involved
● to respond to all needs
● to show respect for the opinions and views of others involved
● to make all feel they are actively involved
● to help provide resources

The activities you select should be safe and stimulating for the children and young people. You may have to consider the following to ensure this:

● whether the setting can afford any resources needed
● that the children are being challenged to an acceptable level by the activity
● that enough staff are available
● that all resources and equipment are safe before use
● the age and stage of development of the children likely to be taking part
● what the children like to do
● any special needs
● any relevant medical details.

It is also important to provide a variety of opportunities that offer choice. There are several reason for this:

● to ensure that each member of the group feels important and valued
● to ensure your play setting is offering quality care that responds appropriately to the needs of the children
● to create a truly child centred play environment that the children want to attend
● to avoid boredom which, in turn, avoids unwanted behaviour.

Plans need to be flexible and to give children the opportunity to create and control play themselves. This is to ensure that:

- play opportunities are child centred
- children feel 'ownership' of the play setting
- children are empowered
- children feel more confident and their self-esteem is enhanced
- decision making and independence are encouraged.

Playworkers can play a vital role in instigating and providing for play. They can provide a range of resources, as shown in the table below.

Resources	Example
Natural materials	Sand, water, clay, puddles, wood, sawdust
Construction materials	Lego, building bricks, stickle bricks, meccano
IT materials and electrical equipment	Computers and games, activity disks, TV, video
Tools	Hammer, screwdriver, saw, craft knife, spade
Outdoor play equipment	Bikes, trolley, swings, climbing frame, seesaw
Craft materials	Collage, boxes, paint, glue, scissors, brushes
Imaginative play materials	Dressing up clothes, jewellery, drapes, tents
Research material	Books, disks, magazines, journals, catalogues
Games and equipment	Board games, footballs, bats and balls
Scrap materials	Empty boxes, tubes, cloth, offcuts of wood

When providing play opportunities an **acceptable level of challenge and risk** should be incorporated. Play workers need to understand the difference between a **risk** and a **hazard** (see pages 70–1). Children need to be equipped to experiment and take risks to help them learn techniques and strategies to deal with risks. However, it is the playworker's responsibility to ensure the safety of children and young people in their care. Supervision and, if necessary, intervention can effectively allow for children to take up challenges and risks.

CASE STUDY

Jon and Desh are in the outside area and have built a den by stacking boxes. They have decided to secure the 'roof' by balancing on the top of the boxes.

1 How would you highlight health and safety rules without stifling play?
2 How could you encourage the imaginative play to continue?

Setting ground rules with and for children and young people

Each setting will have set ground rules for behaviour. These may be included in the setting's behaviour policy (see page 22) and be of a more general nature, focusing on the type of behaviour expected within the setting. Additional ground rules may also be set out at the start of an activity, to focus specifically on the type of activity the children and young people will be engaged in. Ground rules should include boundaries and constraints as well as directives for **appropriate behaviour**. A playworker should focus on positive re-enforcement of these rules, and good practice is to always set the rules with the children and young people. It is important to involve the children in setting the ground rules for the following reasons:

- they will understand the reasoning behind the rules and be more likely to keep to them
- they will understand the rules and hopefully think they are fair
- they will understand why the rules are necessary
- they will learn what rules are for.

You can talk to the children and explain why the ground rules are necessary. Ask them if there are any issues they would like to include, and create a list, ensuring that the reason for the rule is properly discussed and explained. Regularly review and update the list in conjunction with the children. If you are re-negotiating ground rules with the children and young people you must ensure that any changes or adaptations you make to the setting's ground rules are in line with your organisation's policies and procedures. It may help to check the ground rules out with your colleagues or senior playworker.

CONSOLIDATION

1 In the following instances, think about:

- what you would do
- why you would do it
- the resources you would need
- how you would organise it
- how you would set the ground rules
- what opportunities you would make available for free play.

   a You are asked to provide an environmental play opportunity outdoors for a summer play scheme for 15 children.

   b You are asked to become involved in a creative play planning session for children with a range of disabilities.

2 Recall an instance when you provided resources for an activity and discussed the ground rules with the children.

Support children and young people's rights and choices in play

What you need to learn

- Empowering children and young people to exert their rights to choice.
- Balancing children and young people's needs and rights.
- How to identify and support children and young people in play and how to help them adapt play opportunities.
- Responding to the **play cues**.
- Adult interaction in play opportunities.

Empowering children and young people to exert their rights to choice

The Children Act became law in 1989 and the main focus of this Act was to protect children and ensure their rights were upheld. Before the Children Act came into force, the United Nations convention on the rights of the child (1959) gave directives with regard to children's rights, which influenced how children were treated. The wording of the convention is now out-of-date but the ethos (the message) still remains; children have rights and they should be empowered to exert these rights.

Think about it

1 Research into the United Nations convention on the rights of the child and compare it to your own thoughts on children's rights.

2 Look at the Play Values (on pages x–xi) and see which ones relate to children's rights.

The Play Values also relate closely to the rights of children and young people, and as a playworker your role is to incorporate these values into your work practice and help empower children to exert these rights.

Balancing children and young people's needs and rights

In empowering children and young people, a playworker needs to be aware of the need to balance the rights of all the children and young people in the setting. This can involve a range of techniques and strategies, including:

- good listening and communication skills
- an awareness and understanding of equality of opportunity
- a sensitivity to the young people in your care and to their individual needs.

The playwork team can work together to ensure a consistent approach is adopted while still treating children according to their individual needs. If the balance between the individual rights of a child or young person and the rights of others is not addressed, the possible effects could be that the whole group of children suffer as well as individuals, for the following reasons:

- children will not feel valued as individuals
- resentment and jealousy may occur
- health, security and safety directives may be breached
- children may feel neglected
- children may no longer reach their full potential in play, as they feel that the playworkers have favourites or have taken sides.

ACTIVE KNOWLEDGE

Think of an instance when you have used discussion and negotiation to help with ensuring all children's rights are met.

How to identify and support children and young people in play and how to help them adapt play opportunities

At times children and young people will need support in their play, but any support given by the playworker should focus on encouraging independence and getting them to practise skills for themselves. In providing stimulating, interesting and challenging play opportunities that are developmentally appropriate, a playworker is providing the potential for children and young people to extend themselves, as shown in the diagram below.

To assist in all round development

To allow them to explore concepts

To build on the child's natural curiosity

To extend children's knowledge

To hold their interest

Children extend themselves through challenging play opportunities

You, as the playworker, must ensure that the opportunities provided are stimulating and appropriate for the age and stage of development of each child. You should give children and young people choices and involve them in decision making. Being appropriately involved in play will often extend it and gently lead children towards new goals and ideas. Make sure you give support when needed in a sensitive manner.

Support should be provided without the playworker taking control or undermining the child or young person. Support can include things like:

- encouragement and praise
- re-stocking or providing materials and equipment
- physical help with moving, opening or manoeuvring things
- providing information to help with decision making
- pointing out the options available to enable the child to make choices
- negotiating or reiterating ground rules
- highlighting and discussing health, hygiene and safety issues
- acting as mediator in conflict situations
- assessing risks.

Support should be offered but not enforced on the children and young people (except in hazardous situations) and the playworker needs to be aware of withdrawing and being unobtrusive in play.

ACTIVE KNOWLEDGE

Think of an instance when you have provided support by helping children to do any of the suggestions above.

While providing stimulating and challenging environments that offer play opportunities and activities in which children and young people want to participate, a playworker should be sensitive to individual needs by acknowledging that all children are different and have differing needs. By building an appropriate and caring relationship with the children or young people, the playworker will gain their respect and trust. It is important to maintain the relationship by ensuring that you do not undermine their confidence and self-esteem by 'pushing' children and young people too far. It is important for children to explore play opportunities for themselves as it encourages independence, freedom of choice and decision making. Most importantly, it enables them to excel in their own achievements, which will boost their confidence and increase their self-esteem.

Some children and young people are outgoing and need little support or encouragement to take part in play. However, there will be others who may stand on the sideline, looking as though they want to join in, but lacking the confidence to do so. It is your duty as a playworker to help these children gain confidence. This can be achieved in a number of ways:

- play alongside them, giving moral support
- give them assistance, e.g. when walking along a balancing beam, you may hold both hands, then one until the child or young person has the confidence to do it without help

- give a child or young person time and space to try (and to practise) an activity, e.g. learning to skip
- providing praise is a good way to increase a person's self-esteem and confidence
- find out what the child or young person would like to do and, if possible, offer the play opportunity.

ACTIVE KNOWLEDGE

Complete the chart below by indicating the appropriate level of support.

Age	Activity	No support	Little support	Lots of support
5–6 years	Cooking activity			
11–16 years	Game of basketball			
7–8 years	Sewing activity			
11–15 years	Playing computer games			
4–5 years	On a swing			
9–12 years	Making jewellery			
8–10 years	Playing a board game			
15 years	Watching a video			
4–8 years	In the paddling pool			

Discuss your answers with a colleague as you will need to focus on the setting in which you work.

Children and young people require different types of support and encouragement, as shown in the table below.

Age 4–7 years	Age 8–12 years	Age 13+
Children may need lots of additional support with basic skills to help them achieve the desired result. Lots of praise and encouragement is needed to acknowledge effort rather than the end product.	Children may need occasional support but usually only when it is asked for. Can be fiercely independent but usually they respond well to praise and encouragement.	Usually very capable and are unlikely to need direct support. Some discrete assistance may be required from time to time. May appear disdainful of praise, as they fear ridicule from their peers if they respond positively to praise.

Although the table above is directed towards the different age ranges, it is important to balance these with the child or young person's developmental level. The age ranges are only an approximate guide.

ACTIVE KNOWLEDGE

Think about the support and encouragement that you offer to the children and young people in your setting. Then ask yourself these questions:

- Is it asked for?
- Do you volunteer or just barge in?
- Do you withdraw afterwards or do you stay and take over the play opportunity?

Playworkers can improve their practice by becoming reflective practitioners: that is, by thinking back and assessing their practice to identify things that could or should be changed, or by asking colleagues to reflect on their practice (see Unit A52, pages 139–165).

Responding to the play cues

To empower children is to encourage and support them, and the role that you as the playworker should adopt should be sensitive. You need to be aware of the play cues (the verbal language, body language or facial expressions) that children show, which may indicate that they are not happy with a situation. For example a child has been struggling to tie his shoelaces in response to a request to do so before he can go outside to play. His cues will show that he is not happy, is frustrated and is becoming distressed. The playworker should be aware of these cues and assist the child in a way that does not undermine his confidence. The same kind of thing may happen during play and the playworker should be able to pick up cues and act accordingly. The more time that a playworker spends working with children and young people, the more accustomed he or she will become to recognising and acting upon children's play cues.

Play cues can be very varied or very similar. Set responses are recognised especially from children and young people who are:

- related
- spend a lot of time together
- attend the same school or the same class
- live in the same area
- watch the same TV programmes.

Even if the play cues are similar, a playworker should respond to the children according to their individual needs. The playworker's role is a continuous circle:

PLAYWORKER'S CONTINUAL ROLE

TO MONITOR → TO ENCOURAGE → TO SUPPORT → TO OBSERVE → TO ASSESS → TO MONITOR

CASE STUDY

You have a creative table where some of the older children are making masks. You notice that Sam, a 5 year old, is standing watching. He picks up some card and glances round the room, then he catches your eye and quickly puts the card down.

1 How could you respond to this cue?
2 How could you help him join in?
3 How could you support him without undermining his control and involvement?

Adult interaction in play opportunities

There are times when a playworker is required or invited to participate in play opportunities. This may be to join in or to support the children and young people. A playworker should only become involved in play in the following circumstances:

● If invited to by the children and young people. It feels good to be invited to do something and it is a compliment to you if children invite you to play, however, it is important not to take over or stifle their play.

● If the children need help to achieve their aims. This may be physical help, to move or provide something or to collect materials and equipment, or it may be to support children with individual needs to enable them to participate fully.

● To reduce potential hazards and to assess risks. If there is a risk to health, safety or security, your presence may be required. To assess and deal with the issue it is important to encourage the children to try to identify and deal with it themselves, rather than you take over.

● If a conflict situation arises that the children seem unable to resolve. To encourage the children and young people to resolve the conflict themselves is the best course of action and this can often be achieved by negotiation and compromise (you assist as a facilitator if necessary).

● If the children are looking bored and uninterested. Your presence may enthuse and motivate the children and young people, or you could give them an idea to extend or redirect the opportunity.

● During a team game when a team member has to leave. It is important that you do not always win, but be seen to take an active part.

There are times when children and young people would love you to join in, but there are times when your presence will inhibit their play. It is important as a playworker that you are aware of these different requirements.

Only participate in play activities if invited to do so

✔ ACTIVE KNOWLEDGE

Think of the last time you joined in play. Were you invited? Did you meet the guidelines above?

There are times when a playworker should not join in children's play, for a number of reasons, some of which are shown in the diagram below.

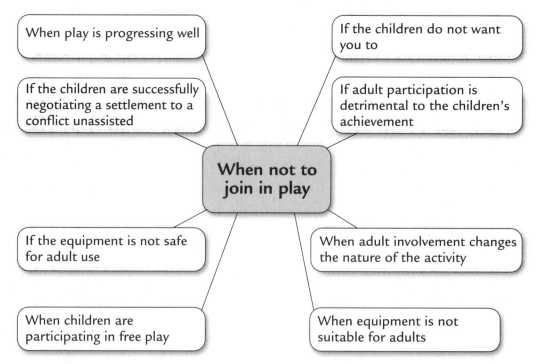

When play is progressing well

If the children do not want you to

If the children are successfully negotiating a settlement to a conflict unassisted

If adult participation is detrimental to the children's achievement

When not to join in play

If the equipment is not safe for adult use

When adult involvement changes the nature of the activity

When children are participating in free play

When equipment is not suitable for adults

CONSOLIDATION

1 A new playworker has become involved in a team game and has become very competitive; the opposing team ask you to join their side. State what you would do and why.

2 Recall an instance when you have responded to a child or young person's play cue and either joined in or not taken part in play.

End play sessions

What you need to learn

- The playworker's role in bringing play sessions to an end.
- The procedures for tidying up the play setting.
- Organisational procedures for children and young people departing the setting.
- Record keeping procedures.

The playworker's role in bringing play sessions to an end

Play opportunities sometimes come to a natural end and this is the best option for the children and young people. They should be encouraged and allowed to complete their play wherever possible. However, there are often times when, and reasons why, play opportunities need to be brought to an end and it is the playworker's role to facilitate (oversee) this in a sensitive and appropriate manner so that the children do not feel disappointed. There are a variety of reasons why play opportunities need to be brought to an end, for example for snack time, to clear away messy creative play, because a parent or carer has arrived for a particular child, or because it is the end of the session.

Play opportunities need to be ended at an appropriate pace for the children participating in them in order to:

- avoid frustration; children will easily become frustrated if their play is terminated while they are busy

- allow children time to complete their tasks and games
- demonstrate that you care about the children and value their play
- encourage them to continue or play again; if children do not complete their play they may refuse to play in the future.

In any of the above situations, it is important to provide the group with a timescale and explanation of how long they have left to complete the activity, why they need to stop what they are doing and, if applicable, when they can pick it up again. If you are able to give a timescale and aim for the activity, the children or young people can adapt their play to accommodate this. Free play opportunities can often be terminated more easily. If a time restraint occurs, the children can change and adapt the activity to meet these deadlines. They can also take a break for lunch or a snack and return to the activity, often without too much disturbance.

Situations sometimes arise that mean you have to break or end the play suddenly. You will need to make contingency plans for these occasions. For example if the activity is outside and the weather changes, space can often be made available indoors unless the activity requires specific equipment and/or a larger space. For emergency evacuation, fire drills and health and safety issues, it is often possible to take a break and return and resume play after the all clear has been given.

The arrival of parents or carers may cause disruption to play, so it is important when planning play activities that this is considered. When a child starts an activity it should be explained that the arrival of parents is at a set time, so they are aware and can plan for this.

CASE STUDY

As it has been raining all afternoon, you organise for the children to watch a video. The children decide to turn the video watching into a 'cinema experience' by putting the chairs in lines and selling pretend tickets and refreshments. By 4 o'clock the video has not finished but several parents and carers have arrived to collect their children.

1 What would you do?
2 How could you have avoided this?

Keys to good practice: Ending play activities

✓ Try to pre-warn children of end times.
✓ Negotiate and discuss end times.
✓ Always give explanations for immediate ends.
✓ Try 'take a break' tactics.
✓ Try and plan for disruptions by having other options available.

✓ **ACTIVE KNOWLEDGE**

List the most usual reasons for ending play sessions at your setting.

Think about it

State the action you would take and explain why you would take this course of action in the following situation:

During the summer the children are outside making a den in the corner of the outdoor space. They start this in the morning and it extends to become a 'camp site'. It is now dinner time and the children need to eat their packed lunches. Play resumes in full by 1 pm and then 20 minutes later it rains.

The procedures for tidying up the play setting

Each setting will have a set policy that involves a tidying up routine and sometimes a rota that staff and children follow for packing away activities. Tidying away will take place as an ongoing process:

- when children and young people move to another activity
- when the area is required for another activity, e.g. snack time
- at the end of an activity
- at the end of the session
- for health and safety reasons, e.g. sweeping up spilt sand.

Most tidying up tasks are appropriate for children or young people to take part in. However, there may be times when the playworker will need to be present, usually for health and safety reasons, for example when washing sharp knives. Tidying up is an important part of development for children and young people, so that they understand the importance of leaving the areas clean and tidy and ready for the next person to use. Development areas include the following:

Social skills such as:

- working together to achieve the task
- co-operating with others
- improving self-help skills and independence
- sharing ideas with others as to how to do it as quickly as possible
- acting in a socially acceptable manner.

Physical skills such as:

- eye to hand coordination
- fine and gross motor skills.

Children and young people should be involved in tidying up for the reasons given in the diagram below.

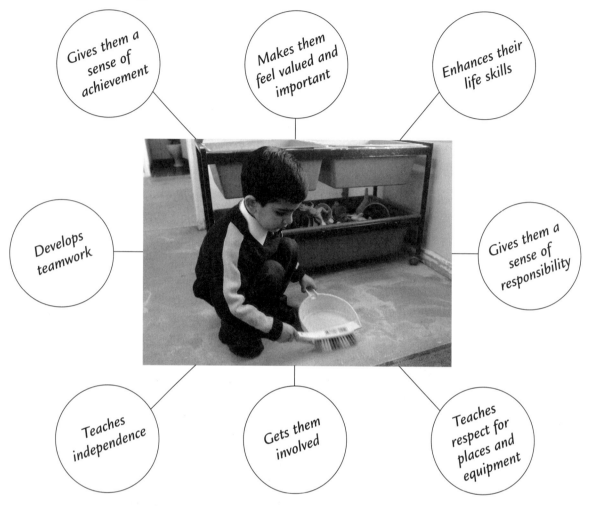

Why involve children and young people in tidying up?

While it is appropriate for children and young people to tidy up after themselves, this will be dependent on:

- the age, size and development of the children or young people
- the type of materials and equipment, and where they are stored
- the risks involved, e.g. high shelves need to be assessed before enlisting the help of children and young people.

CASE STUDY

After an afternoon visit to the local farm, you return to the play setting with an hour left before parents and carers are due to arrive to collect their children. The children start drawing and making animals on the creative table.

1 How could you bring the session to an end?
2 How could you get feedback on the activity?
3 How would you ensure the activity is tidied away?

The procedures that you follow in your setting will have been established, taking into account the type of setting in which you work, the storage space available and the number of staff available. Clearing away usually takes place when the children and young people have vacated the premises, but this will depend upon the hours the staff are expected to work.

Keys to good practice: Tidying up

✓ Encourage children to help with tidying up.
✓ Move only small equipment until children have gone.
✓ Ensure you have enough staff.
✓ Move children to another area.

ACTIVE KNOWLEDGE

Think about the equipment you have at your setting that the children and young people can tidy away themselves. Is it always the same children or young people that do it?

Organisational procedures for children and young people departing the setting

It is very important that, as playworkers, you are aware of children leaving the site, whether the setting operates an open or closed access. Generally, in open access settings, the children or young people are encouraged to sign in and out, for health and safety and legal reasons. In closed access settings, children are not allowed to leave the building without a designated parent or carer, who should be listed on their registration form. The parent or carer would normally sign their child out of a setting.

The DfES guidelines state that arrangements should be made with parents about the arrival and departure of their children to and from the provision, and staff should make sure that they are collected by the correct person. The guidelines also state that children should be released from the provision to individuals named by the parent only.

ACTIVE KNOWLEDGE

1 Check out your policies for children and young people leaving the setting. If you are a closed access scheme compare them to the DfES standards.
2 Imagine that you are working in a play setting. One day a woman appears and says that she has come to collect Pamjit. She tells you that she is Pamjit's aunty and that Pamjit's mum has sent her. What would you do? Would you let Pamjit go with the woman?

Record keeping procedures

The Children Act (1989) set out requirements regarding the records that settings are required to keep, which include the following:

- a daily attendance register to indicate clearly the children present at any given time
- current information on all children, to be reviewed regularly and include details of medical and dietary requirements plus emergency contact details
- accident/incident books
- staff/volunteer records.

Most settings adhere to this and often keep other records that will be of benefit to the children and young people and to the setting.

Throughout a session a number of records may be made, for example:

- The register will be completed on arrival and again on departure. This is a very important document and must be kept up-to-date for legal as well as health and safety reasons.
- Any accidents or illnesses that occur and any medication administered during the session need to be written up in the accident book, and the parents or carers informed.
- Any incidents should be noted. The setting usually has one book for positive or negative behaviour, and one for health and safety monitoring (e.g. faulty equipment, appliances that need checking etc.).
- Items bought with petty cash or grants need to be recorded, as well as payments from parents or carers for the service of the setting.
- Fire drills need to be recorded; this will be done on a legal document that includes details of when the fire fighting equipment was checked.

When children and young people join a setting, personal records are set up that provide the staff with the necessary information should an emergency arise. These records also inform the staff of any medical conditions or allergies that the children may have. Once all records are complete, they must then be locked away and stored in a secure cabinet. Access to children's files is limited. All records that are kept should be accurate and legible so that, if and when they are required, they can be easily read and understood.

✓ **ACTIVE KNOWLEDGE**

Find out what records your setting keeps and how they are stored.

CONSOLIDATION

1 Recall an instance when you have been involved in:
- bringing a play opportunity to an end
- the process of children leaving the setting
- keeping records.

END OF UNIT TEST

1 List two ways you can obtain feedback from children and young people on what they want in the play environment.

2 Give four examples of equipment suitable for young people aged 12 – 16 years.

3 Suggest some materials that you would make available to encourage free play outside.

4 Explain why children and young people should be involved in creating play environments and how you would go about involving them.

5 Describe the types of support that children and young people might need to adapt to a play opportunity and how you might provide this support without taking control.

6 How would you identify if and when children and young people need support during a play opportunity?

7 Explain how to bring a play session to an end in a way that respects the children and young people's needs and involvement, but meets the requirements of your play setting.

8 Describe your organisation's procedures for children and young people's departure.

Contribute to the health and safety of the play environment

The role of a playworker is to provide an environment where children and young people feel physically and emotionally safe. As a playworker, it is your responsibility to ensure the play environment – the premises, the play resources and the activities – is free from hazards. You should also encourage the participants in your care to gain knowledge and experience to maintain their own safety.

This unit is divided into two elements:

● PW3.1 Maintain the health and safety of the play environment users.
● PW3.2 Maintain the health, safety and welfare of children and young people during play.

The Play Values covered in this unit are shown below:

Value No	Statement
4	An environment must be provided that stimulates and provides opportunities for risks and challenges, and growth of confidence and self-esteem.
5	A play environment must be provided in which children feel physically and personally safe and able to take part in activities free from hazards.
7	As a playworker, you should be considerate and caring.
11	Play opportunities should be provided within the current legislative framework.

Children and young people have the right to play in environments that do not cause harm to their health, safety and welfare. It is an important part of a playworker's responsibility to ensure that the environment both indoors and outside is hazard free, but still provides levels of challenge and risk that will stimulate the children to play and develop.

The reasons why playworkers need to be alert to health, safety and **security hazards** are shown in the table overleaf.

If playworkers are constantly vigilant about safety and **hygiene hazards**, the following will occur:

● parents or carers will have peace of mind and confidence in the play setting
● children and young people will feel safe in the setting and with the adults who are there with them
● emergencies will be avoided, injuries and damage will be prevented
● children will be prevented from playing on equipment that is damaged or broken
● there will be less likelihood of cross infection or spread of infection
● the setting will meet the standards set by the inspecting body and meet legal requirements.

Reasons	Examples
To prevent accidents that could result in injury	If a drink is spilt on the floor and not cleaned up
To prevent cross infection	Milk left uncovered in a warm temperature
To abide by legislation	Fire exits locked or blocked
To make sure that equipment meets safety requirements	Broken or damaged toys set out for use
To stop the spread of infection	Toilet areas that are not cleaned regularly
To stop children wandering off	Outside gates not securely fastened
To prevent intruders	Doors and entrances without security locks
To uphold the maintenance of the building	Windows left open and banging in the wind
Children only leave the setting with the correct people	An 'auntie' to collect without prior notice
To avoid emergencies	Toxic fumes from glue

Vigilance about safety hazards will enhance the quality of the provision you provide and the setting's reputation will be upheld.

While it is important for the play setting to be hazard free, the children and young people still need to be challenged and stimulated, as learning through play involves understanding and dealing with risks. A playworker needs to be able to distinguish and be clear about the differences between a hazard and a risk.

A hazard is something within a play setting that has the potential to cause someone harm, for example not cleaning up a spilt drink or equipment left blocking fire exits. It is the playworker's responsiblity to ensure the safety of the children in his or her care.

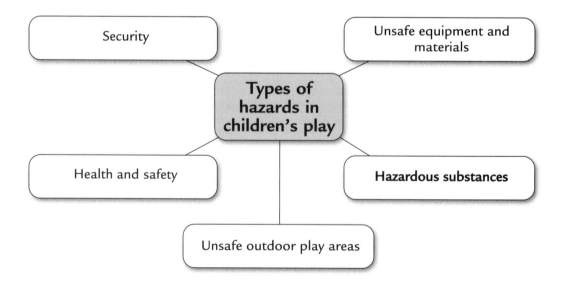

A risk is a potential danger. The chance of the danger happening can be minimised by you as the playworker, for example a climbing frame can be a hazardous piece of equipment if a child were to fall from it and hurt itself. However, if the climbing frame is checked before use, complies with health and safety standards and is only used under supervision, then it becomes an acceptable risk rather than a hazard.

✓ ACTIVE KNOWLEDGE

1 Look around your play setting for risks and hazards. See if you can identify three of each.
2 Try the exercise below and tick the correct box.

Example	Risk	Hazard
An activity is set up in front of the fire exit doors		
The children are cutting out card using sharp scissors		
A broken bottle is on the grass outside		
A vegetable knife is provided for cutting carrots		
Cleaning fluids are kept on top of the low level toilet cistern		
A playworker is with a group of children making kites from polythene bags		

When a playworker applies for a position, the job description sent out will almost certainly involve clauses about health and safety for which you will be expected to provide evidence in your application or during the interview. An example is shown below:

General duties and responsibilities:
● To support and participate in initiatives to ensure a safe and healthy environment for all the setting's users.

Personal specifications:
● Be able to demonstrate awareness of health and safety issues.

Think about it

If you were being interviewed and asked to demonstrate an awareness of health and safety issues, what examples would you give?

Guidelines and legislation are set out for inspection, and each setting should abide by the National Standards for out of school care with regard to health and safety and welfare.

Standard 7: Health and safety

- **Health:** The registered person promotes the good health of children and takes positive steps to prevent the spread of infection and appropriate measures if they are ill.
- **Hygiene:** The premises and equipment are clean. The registered person ensures that staff are informed and aware of the importance of good hygiene practice in order to prevent the spread of infection. Staff are informed of and kept up-to-date with hygiene procedures.
- **Animals:** The registered person ensures that any animals on the premises are safe to be in the proximity of children and do not pose a health risk.
- **Food handling:** Those responsible for the preparation and handling of food are fully aware of, and comply with, regulations relating to food safety and hygiene.
- **Medicine:** The registered person has a clear policy, understood by all staff and discussed with parents, regarding the administration of medication. If medicine is to be given, it includes the following:
  - medicines are stored in their original containers, clearly labelled and inaccessible to children
  - medicines are not usually administered unless they have been prescribed for the child by a doctor
  - the parent gives prior written permission to administer any medication
  - written records are kept of all medicines administered to children, and parents sign the record book to acknowledge the entry
  - if the administration of prescription medicines requires technical or medical knowledge then individual training is provided for staff from a qualified health professional. Training is specific to the individual child concerned.
- **First aid:** There is a first aid box complying with health and safety (first aid) regulations (1981), the contents of which are checked frequently and replaced as necessary by a designated member of staff. It is kept in an accessible place out of reach of children. There is at least one member of staff with a current first aid training certificate on the premises or on outings at any one time. The first aid qualification includes training in first aid for infants and young children.

The National Standards also recommend that the physical environment for the children should have adequate space, which welcomes children and provides a range of activities that will promote their development.

Standard 4: Physical environment

- The premises are made welcoming and friendly to children and parents.
- The premises are clean, well lit, adequately ventilated, and maintained in a suitable state of repair and decoration.
- The rooms used for out of school care are for the sole use of the facility during the hours of operation.
- The registered person ensures they operate within local planning and building control requirements.

- There is access to a telephone on the premises.
- Rooms are maintained at an adequate temperature.

Indoor activity area
- The space standards provide minimum space requirements for the whole provision. The registered person shows how this space will be divided up and used to provide activities for children and how staff will be deployed within it. There is a minimum of 2.3 square metres of space per child.
- Provision is made (space or partitioned area) for children who wish to relax or play quietly, equipped with appropriate furniture. This area may be converted from normal play space provided children can rest safely without disturbance.
- Play areas are large enough to give scope for free movement and well spread out activities. There are separate areas for different activities.
- There is adequate storage space for equipment.

Outdoor activity area
- If outdoor play space adjoining the premises is provided, it is safe, secure and well maintained.

Each setting will have its own **health and safety policies and procedures** to ensure the welfare of children and young people, and these should be readily available to all staff, parents, carers and other interested bodies. They will include examples such as those in the table below.

Example	Explanation
Health and hygiene	Prevent the spread of infection and maintain the cleanliness of the setting
Outdoor play	Frequency of outdoor opportunity
Food handling	Implementing legislation for food hygiene
Cleaning and clearing	Procedures to prevent the spread of infection
Medicines	Procedures for storing, administering and recording
First aid	Training given, procedures and policies for administering first aid
Accidents	Procedures for recording and responding responsibly
Hazardous substances	Records of where these are kept and why
Evacuation practices	Fire drills etc.
Equipment	Procedures to ensure quality and upkeep meet manufacturer's guidelines
Environment	Hazard free, both indoors and outside
Entrances	The entrance has a security system
Outdoor play	Good gates and fences
Collection of children	Strict policies and procedures as to who is allowed to collect children
Lost child	Clear procedures should a child get lost
Staff	Staff police checks
Behavioural policy	Description of behaviour guidelines and boundaries
Child protection	Policy and procedures established

✓ **ACTIVE KNOWLEDGE**

Look at your setting's policies and see if all the suggestions in the table on page 73 are included.

All playworkers have the responsibility of providing a safe and secure environment for the children and young people in their care. It is your duty to abide by the policies and procedures of the setting and the legislation on working with children. The consequences for not complying with legislation include:

- closure of the setting by an inspecting body
- parents or carers losing confidence in the setting and withdrawing their children
- personal implications with regard to police involvement and prosecution.

The main legislation that relates to health, safety and security in the play setting is the Health and Safety Act (1974). All environments must comply with the regulations set by this Act. It is important that senior staff keep up-to-date with this Act and pass on relevant information to those who work for them.

The Act states that employers must:

- provide a safe working environment
- abide by health and safety polices
- complete a risk assessment on the premises
- provide training for staff
- ensure equipment follows safety guidelines.

The Act states that employees must:

- know and implement health and safety policies
- use safety equipment and protection according to set guidelines
- never place themselves or others at risk as a result of their own practice.

Because this Act became legislation in 1974, the health and safety executive has since set regulations that each setting is required to follow. The setting will be checked at inspection and if there has been a breach of the regulations resulting in an injury, potential injury or death, this will be investigated by the health and safety executive and will usually lead to prosecution.

Regulations	Checked by	Details
First Aid Regulation (1981)	Inspectorate, Health and Safety Executive	Legal requirements to provide a first aid box, qualified first aider and first aid records. Report serious accidents to the health and safety executive.
Control of Substances Hazardous to Health and Safety Regulations (COSHH) (2003)	Inspectorate, Health and Safety Executive	Employers to assess use of all hazardous substances. They must be stored safely, ensuring instructions are followed, and protective clothing should be provided and used.
Reporting of Injuries, Diseases and Dangerous Occurrences Regulations (RIDDOR) (1995)	Inspectorate, Health and Safety Executive, Environmental Health	Detailed records to be kept (accident book) and reported to Health and Safety Executive/Environmental Health within seven days. Injuries that stop employers working for more than three days should be reported.
The fire precautions (work place) regulations (1997)	Local Fire Officer	Fire departments give free advice on these regulations. Fire safety officers will check premises for evacuation routines and routes, fire fighting equipment, electrical safety and storage of flammable materials.
Transport Act (1985)	Ministry of Transport	Drivers must be over 21 years and have a full licence and insurance. Seat belts and MOT will be required. It is the driver's responsibility to check the mini bus/car before each journey.
Safety standards for toys and equipment	Inspectorate	Toys and equipment should carry the CE/Kite mark/Lion mark to comply with British Safety Standards.
Food Safety Act (1990)	Inspectorate, Environmental Health	Advice and guidance provided by Environmental Health. Basic food hygiene certificate recommended. Any illness that may have been caused by contamination to be reported to the Local Environmental Health Department.
Insurance employer and public liability	Inspectorate, Health and Safety Executive	The Children Act (1989) recommends that settings have public liability to cover accidents and injuries that may occur.

Safety standards for toys and equipment

The Lion mark shows that toys conform to British Standard 5665. It is a mark of the safety and quality of a toy, used by members of the British Toy and Hobby Manufacturers Association only.

The CE mark is a declaration by the manufacturer or its authorised representative that the product complies with the essential requirements laid down in the corresponding European Union Directive(s).

The Kite mark shows that the product samples have been tested by the British Standards Institution (BSI) and have been assessed against a quality system (BSEN ISO 9000). The BSI continually monitor products and production to ensure that toys and equipment continue to meet the standards.

Strict regulations cover equipment, and when playworkers buy products it is important to check that they confirm to the required regulation. Remember, you must follow the manufacturer's guidelines and instructions when setting out and preparing equipment. It may help to keep these guidelines in an accessible place.

The other important legislation in maintaining children's health, safety and security is the Children Act (1989), which was introduced to ensure childcare settings were regulated. This Act contains information for providing a safe and secure environment. It gives local authorities the duty to ensure that settings are inspected and that the inspection meets the DfES standards. The inspections are now carried out by OfSTED (Office for Standards in Education) for all settings that care for children less than 8 years old for more than a two-hour period. Health, hygiene, safety and security are checked during this inspection and an action plan is set to help improve the setting's practice and policies. Settings with action plan points are monitored to ensure these are effectively implemented.

It is important that children and young people learn personal survival skills. These skills will help them cope in certain situations. One way of introducing or maintaining this is to encourage them to be aware of the health, safety and security hazards in the setting, and to give them strategies and techniques to help them deal with these hazards. It is important to encourage children and young people to be aware of health, safety and security hazards for the following reasons:

- for their own safety and wellbeing
- it teaches them to be independent
- it teaches them to care for others
- to help them take responsibility for their actions
- to make them feel secure
- to improve their self-help skills
- to help them think about the safety of others
- it makes them feel grown up
- to raise awareness of health and safety issues
- to promote self-esteem and self-confidence.

Encouraging children and young people to take some responsibility for their own health and safety will help their social development and encourage a more caring nature. A playworker is in a good position to promote health and safety and encourage the children and young people to take responsibility by:

- being a positive role model
- highlighting and explaining hazards
- offering options and advice with regard to coping with issues
- supporting children and young people to find solutions themselves
- providing activities and opportunities that highlight the types of hazards they may encounter
- giving praise and encouragement for the effort to deal with health, safety and security issues, to build confidence
- reiterating ground rules
- explaining the different consequences for a range of actions.

✓ ACTIVE KNOWLEDGE

Think of all the things that could result in health and safety issues in your setting. How many of these could the children and young people take responsibility for?

Examples of activities where children can take risks are shown in the table below:

Activity	Risk to assess
Cutting out	How to minimise the risk of cutting fingers.
Climbing frame	How to minimise the risk of falling, how high up is it safe to go, where are the hand and footholds.
Cooking	How to minimise the risk of cuts, burns and scalds, how sharp is the knife, where to cut safely, how to hold the pan/tin in the oven, where to put the tin afterwards.

By talking about potentially dangerous situations and discussing options, playworkers can help children and young people to become confident in their ability to judge risks and take the necessary actions to minimise accidents.

Maintain the health and safety of the play environment users

What you need to learn

- Routine health and safety checks.
- Risk assessment in the play setting.
- The types of hazards that are likely to occur in the play environments.

Routine health and safety checks

Each setting's health and safety policy will give advice and guidelines on how to assess and deal with health, hygiene, safety and security issues and incidents. The aspects of your policy that you should know about are shown in the diagram below.

Where policies and procedures are kept

How they are introduced

How they are implemented within the setting

What they say

What records are kept

How often they are updated

Get to know your setting's health and safety policy

It is of no use to know where the polices are and what the polices say unless you implement then. Implementation will involve things like:

- health and safety checks
- record keeping
- promoting good practice
- attending training sessions to update your skills and knowledge
- dealing with hazardous situations as they occur
- intervening before risks become hazards
- being a positive role model
- completing a risk assessment.

Part of a playworker's role will be to carry out health and safety checks on a regular basis. Some checks against **health, safety and welfare incidents** will be more formal and will need to be recorded, whereas other checks will be informal and will involve playworkers using common sense in identifying hazards. For example if you see a child skipping outside with their shoe laces undone, you would automatically tell them that their shoe laces are undone so they can tie them up (or you can help them) in order to prevent an accident.

Routine health and safety checks can be carried out daily, weekly, monthly or termly, and will focus on things such as:

- the building
- the outdoor area
- toys and activities
- equipment and materials.

By carrying out routine health and safety checks in the play environment, you can minimise unacceptable risks. Some settings devise checklists to help focus on set things, as shown on page 81.

✓ ACTIVE KNOWLEDGE

1 Ask to see the health and safety checklist at your setting. Compare it to the one on page 81. Highlight things to add to your list.
2 Were you given information on health and safety at your induction? If not, ask a colleague/senior worker to explain the process to you.

Things to check	Dates	Things to check	Dates
Toilet area:		**Kitchen area:**	
Bins emptied and with lids		Fridge temperature	
Floor surfaces		Food storage	
Tissues/toilet paper		Sell by/use by date	
Soap		Linen change	
Dryer working		Fire fighting equipment	
Paper towels		Cleanliness	
Indoor play area:		**First aid box:**	
Ventilation		Contents	
Heating		Accident book available	
Cleanliness		Storage of medication	
Fire fighting equipment			
Tables and chairs			
Toys and equipment			
Entrance:		**Outside play area:**	
Security buzzer working		Fences and gates secure	
Locks/bolts working		Free from glass	
Visitor's book		Free from debris	
		Free from litter	
		Surfaces safe	
Fire evacuation details:			
Visible notice			
Fire fighting equipment			
Fire door working			
Clear access			
Initials of person carrying out check:			

In every setting, recording and maintaining health, hygiene, safety and security is a necessity for the following reasons:

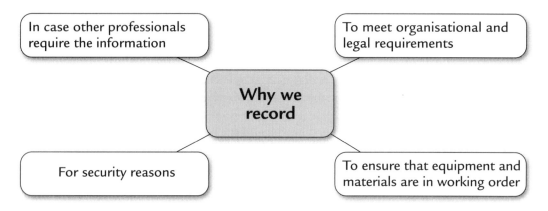

The things you should record in the play setting are shown in the table below.

Item	Where to record
Accidents and injuries	Accident book
Illnesses/medical conditions	Illness book
Attendance	Register
Fire evacuation drills	Fire book
Fire alarm tests	Fire book
Fire equipment tests	Fire book
Incidents	Incident book
Children's details	Children's file
Emergency contact details	Personal file
Health and safety checks	Health and safety book
Risk assessments	Health and safety book
Visitors to the setting	Visitors book

✔ ACTIVE KNOWLEDGE

Check the things that are recorded in your setting. Ensure you are aware of your responsibilities in completing written records and that you know the details of what to include.

Risk assessment in the play setting

A risk assessment is a person's own judgement in exposing a possible danger. To assess risks you have to consider:

- the consequences of something happening
- the likelihood of it happening.

As a playworker, you will be constantly vigilant and will be **assessing risk** consciously and subconsciously throughout the working day. The earlier example of the shoelace that was undone was a hazard, and the playworker completed a risk assessment on the possible dangers that could occur while the child was skipping. Another example would be if you had something stored on a high shelf and you needed it in a hurry – should you use a chair or fetch the steps?

In some instances, you may need to complete more formal risk assessments for activities or opportunities that you offer children and young people. These are usually in written form and your setting will have a format for them.

ACTIVE KNOWLEDGE
Ask your senior playworker how the setting carries out risk assessments.

Keys to good practice: How to carry out a risk assessment

✓ Look around your work place (indoors and outside) to see what could cause harm to a child or young person in your care.

✓ Is the risk from the hazard minimal, e.g. chairs stacked appropriately and turned towards a wall to prevent them from falling into the play area?

✓ Check the health and safety procedures of your setting. Make sure any risk assessments are written down, e.g. socket covers are used when sockets are not in use.

✓ Review your health and safety procedures and amend if necessary.

ACTIVE KNOWLEDGE
Walk around your setting (indoors and outside) and make a list of things that might cause harm to a child or young person.

The types of hazards that are likely to occur in the play environments

Look at the picture below. Can you spot all the hazards and potential hazards?

In a play environment, there will be many types of hazards. Some will be more obvious and will be dealt with as a matter of course. Others will be less obvious. Playworkers usually carry out checks at the beginning of a session, but some hazards will appear during the session and will need to be dealt with as they emerge.

The causes of risks can be minimised by the playworkers being vigilant and assessing potential dangers (risk assessment). You will be able to deal with some hazards yourself; some you will need help with; others you will need to report to a senior playworker.

For some hazards, you may need to isolate the hazard (cordon it off so that children cannot get near to it). Remember, if unsure or in doubt:

- seek support
- ask for advice
- refer to and check policies and procedures
- complete relevant records.

Your senior playworker will guide you through the process.

Dealing with hazards

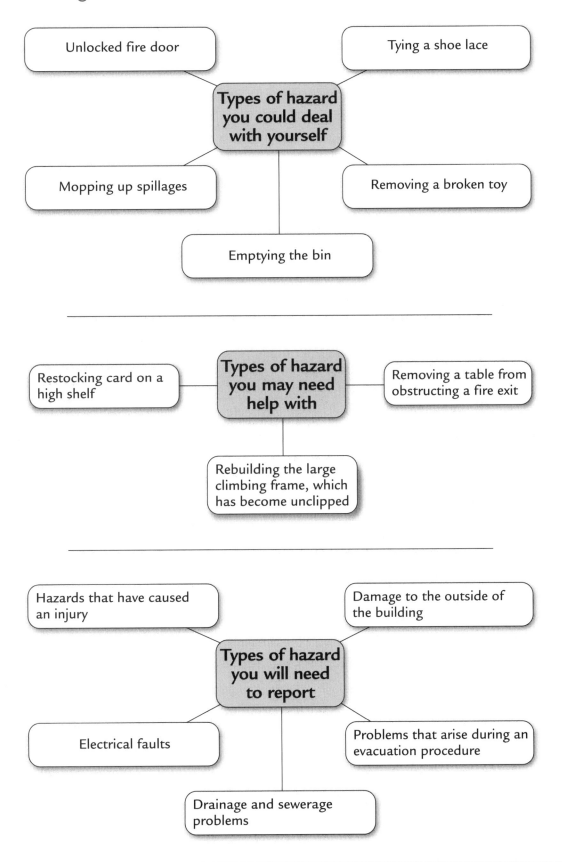

Types of hazard you could deal with yourself
- Unlocked fire door
- Tying a shoe lace
- Mopping up spillages
- Removing a broken toy
- Emptying the bin

Types of hazard you may need help with
- Restocking card on a high shelf
- Removing a table from obstructing a fire exit
- Rebuilding the large climbing frame, which has become unclipped

Types of hazard you will need to report
- Hazards that have caused an injury
- Damage to the outside of the building
- Electrical faults
- Problems that arise during an evacuation procedure
- Drainage and sewerage problems

In all workplaces, hazards will occur. No environment will be risk free. A playworker should:

- identify the risks and hazards
- assess the potential dangers
- think how to minimise the risks
- act accordingly.

Types of hazard	How to assess the risk	How to minimise the risk
Sand spilt on floor from the indoor sand tray.	Visually check, can people slip and fall?	Act by ensuring the sand is swept up and put in a bucket to be washed.
The sun is shining through the window making the TV hard to see, so a child has moved the TV to one side and the wire is trailing.	Visually check, is the wire where children could be walking? Could someone trip over it?	Act by closing the curtains/blinds or turning the TV. Return the TV to its original safe position.
The hand drier in the toilet area has broken and children need to dry their hands.	Check the drier. Turn it off/unplug it. Ensure the drier is safe. Think what else children could use.	Report the breakdown of the drier. Provide paper towels and a bin with a lid to stop cross infection.
In the outdoor play area, the fence has been damaged and a piece of wood is sticking out.	Visually check, is the fence damaged enough for intruders/animals to get in? Is the wood a potential danger?	Report the damage. Try and remove the wood if you are able to and if it is a danger. Cordon off the area. Secure the boundary fence.

4 You are supervising a group of young people aged 12–15 years. You have organised an off-site activity and have hired bicycles. One of the bicycles looks like this:

CONSOLIDATION

1 Think of times when you have:
- identified and dealt with a hazard in the play setting
- encouraged children to identify and report hazards
- completed a risk assessment
- minimised the risk for a potential danger
- completed records relating to hazardous situations.

For each example, explain what you did and why you did it. These could be recorded as a reflective account or a diary sheet.

2 Next time you deal with a hazard, ask someone to witness your actions. You can then get a witness statement completed.

3 Describe and explain a time when you isolated a hazard and reported it to a senior colleague.

Maintain the health, safety and welfare of children and young people during play

What you need to learn

- How to ensure children and young people are safe when playing alone.
- How to judge how much supervision to give during play.
- How to judge when behaviour is causing unacceptable levels of risk.

How to ensure children and young people are safe when playing alone

Play is at its best when it is spontaneous and freely chosen by the children and young people involved. An adult may be required to provide equipment and materials or to help if invited, but child-led play is the most satisfying for children.

You cannot wrap children up in cotton wool. They need to learn how to cope with dangerous situations in everyday life, such as crossing roads, stranger danger and substances that are harmful to health.

As a playworker, you need to be a good role model and provide opportunities, discussion and advice that will enable a child or young person to gain an understanding of ways to maintain their own safety. This will also boost their confidence, and encourage them to be aware of their own and other's safety and to report any hazards they may come across while playing.

In order for a child or young person to gain the most from a play opportunity and maintain safety, he or she needs to learn and understand the boundaries of the activity and why they are important; e.g. in a scavenger hunt for natural objects, the participants will need to know that they cannot touch some plants such as daffodils, as they are poisonous. The children will also need to know the boundaries and timescale they have to collect the items on the list.

Playworkers are in a unique position to provide information and advice about health, safety and security that will help ensure the wellbeing and welfare of the children and young people.

Each setting will have its own code of behaviour (or ground rules). The most effective way of setting this up is to involve the children and young people, since this will give them ownership of the guidelines and boundaries for acceptable and unacceptable behaviour (see page 19). Ground rules are important for the children's physical safety as well as their health and wellbeing. They also help the smooth running of the setting and help children to become aware of dangerous behaviour.

Although the setting will have an established code of behaviour, a playworker will need to remind children of, and reinforce, the ground rules on many occasions.

Before an activity begins

A playworker will need to reinforce ground rules

When new equipment or materials are introduced

When observing potentially dangerous play

ACTIVE KNOWLEDGE

1 Imagine you have a new piece of equipment – an extra large ball about a metre in diameter. You unpack it with the children. Would you:

● sit them all down and say, 'No fighting over it, no pushing each other, no playing on the slope with it, no throwing it at each other',

or

● suggest that they discuss the type of guidelines needed to help with safety when playing with the ball.

2 Which response would be the most useful for the children?

Children's memories develop at different levels, so it may be that you need to remind some children more than you do others of the types of behaviour that are safe. Remember to focus on the behaviour and why this is potentially dangerous rather than on the child or young person. For example, you could say, 'Please be careful when making the sandwich, the knife could easily cut you or someone else', rather than, 'Don't do that, you are always doing dangerous things'. The tone of voice that you use and the way you phrase things will help children to adopt a similar manner.

Information about health and safety issues can be effectively passed on to children and young people by activities that involve instances of potential danger. A copy of a picture showing hazards in the home, garden or play setting could be used to this effect. An example is given below.

What are the potential dangers?

Children and young people could be asked to identify the hazards in the picture. This is an excellent opportunity to discuss issues around health and safety. Other ways of providing safety information to children are shown in the spider diagram on the opposite page.

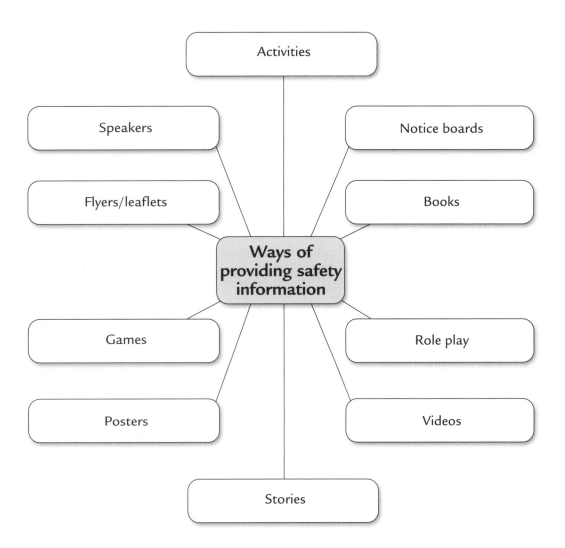

How to judge how much supervision to give during play

Local authorities and inspecting bodies set staff ratios (the number of staff required for a set number of children) to help ensure children's safety and wellbeing. The type of play setting you are in will determine the number of staff to child ratio, but there is always a minimum of two adults on duty.

- In open access schemes, which have children aged between 5 and 7 years, the minimum staffing ratio is 1:3.
- Schemes running in public parks may have a higher staffing ratio; you would need to speak to you local OfSTED advisor for clarification.
- Day care settings, such as after school clubs (closed access), with children aged 3–8 years, have a minimum staffing ratio of 1:8.

✓ **ACTIVE KNOWLEDGE**

Think about how many children you have in your setting and how many staff you have working. Look at the staff ratios.

To help keep children safe, the role of the playworker is to supervise their play. Playworkers need to be vigilant during supervision, as dangerous situations can occur suddenly. You need to use your common sense and observation skills to enable intervention at the right time and in the correct manner. In this way, you will not frighten the child but help them to assess the risk before it is taken. It is important to avoid over protection. Not allowing the child or young person to take any risks can be frustrating and smothering for the child, and will inhibit their play. Children need to be allowed to take on limited responsibility for their safety, and this will involve an element of risk.

There are several ways of supervising children, but the three levels shown in the table below are the most frequently used within a play setting.

Level of supervision	What it means in practice	Example
General observation	Being able to see what children and young people are doing, possibly from a distance.	Children are allowed to play on the grass while you are on the other side of the area, with children who are playing with bats and balls.
Close supervision	Close at hand, focusing on the children's activities but not being directly involved in what they are doing, allowing them to assess potential risks and hazards.	Supervising a craft activity, on hand to re-stock materials and answer queries and requests.
Constant supervision	Being with the children all the time, usually in a supporting role. Often being involved in the activity.	Supporting children using scissors or knives, you sit with them all the time.

While you may be offering supervision to an individual or a small group, it is important to be aware of what is happening in other parts of the environment. This may mean that you position yourself so you can see the other activities and not have your back to them or the door.

Some children may need more supervision, at a more intense level, than others. Your understanding of the children in your care and their development needs will prove an asset when assessing the type of supervision required. You may have children and young people in your care with additional needs. Your role is to support inclusion. You should allow children and young people opportunities regardless of their needs, and support and encourage their participation. It is important not to be over-protective, but to allow them space and opportunities to assess and take risks while still ensuring their safety and wellbeing.

Complete the box below by entering ticks in the boxes you think are most appropriate for the level of supervision required.

Activity	General	Close	Constant
A 5 year old making a sandwich with a butter knife.			
A 9 year old making a collage picture.			
A 14 year old using a computer.			
A group of 8–9 year olds making a den.			

How to judge when behaviour is causing unacceptable levels of risk

When supervising children you will become aware of instances when your supervision will need to be more constant. This will be when play and children's behaviour may cause harm to health, safety and wellbeing.

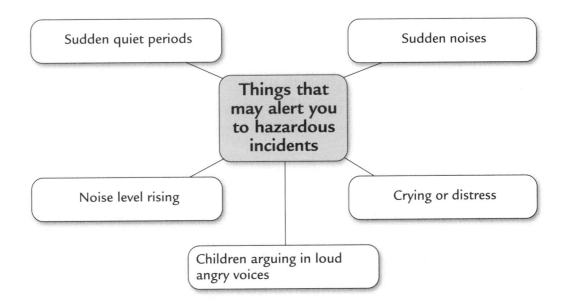

Children's play can start off quite tame, but can rapidly increase to boisterous play as they become excited. As you become more experienced in your setting, you will be aware of the usual noise level and any deviations from it will alert you. You may glance over to check what is happening or need to move to see. You will need to assess the situation and decide whether the children can sort the problem out for themselves or whether they need support, such as a mediator. The types of play and behaviour that may cause you concern are shown in the table overleaf.

Causes for concern	Example
Equipment being used for the wrong purposes	Using scissors as a hammer or screwdriver
Equipment being used by children of the wrong size/age	A 10-year-old on a seesaw which is suitable for children up to 5 years old
Aggressive behaviour	Children using sticks as weapons
Loud argumentative voices	Children shouting and snatching toys
Overexcited voices	Children discovering another child squirting water
Sudden loud noises	A child reaching up to get something and it falling
Exclamations of distress or crying	A child who has trapped his finger

The ability to judge if a situation is becoming, or has become, hazardous, develops as you become more experienced. Dangerous situations can develop rapidly, so playworkers need to be able to identify potential, as well as actual, problems.

Action often needs to be taken quickly to avoid accidents, but disruption to children's play can mean that the play stops and opportunities are lost. A sensitive approach to disrupting play should be adopted. However, if the behaviour or stage of play is potentially dangerous, and a child or young person is at risk, play should be stopped immediately and an explanation given as to why it has been stopped.

CASE STUDY

Before you go outside with the children and young people you notice that there is a carrier bag with something in it on the grass. You also see that the gate is open.

1 What action would you take?
2 What records would you complete?

Keys to good practice: Assessing risk

✓ Always follow your setting's policies and procedures.
✓ Keep within the legal guidelines, assess risks and act accordingly.
✓ Record and report all incidents.

What action would you take in the following scenarios?

- A 10-year-old wants to plug in a stereo which has a loose wire and gave out a couple of sparks yesterday.
- A 14-year-old wants to use a ladder to climb on the roof to get a ball.

CONSOLIDATION

1 Plan, implement and evaluate an activity to raise children's awareness of health, safety and wellbeing.

2 Record instances when you have:
- given information on health and safety before children play
- encouraged children to take responsibility for their own health and safety
- supported children in their play by identifying risks.

3 Recall an instance when you have taken action when children are playing to minimise a risk or avert a dangerous situation. Remember to say why you did what you did (your rationale) and how you recorded the incident.

END OF UNIT TEST

1 State the importance of children and young people being able to play in an environment that does not cause harm to their health, safety, and welfare, whilst still providing levels of challenge and risk that will help them to play and develop.

2 List your responsibilities for ensuring the health, safety and welfare of children and young people under relevant current legislation.

3 Describe the types of hazards that are likely to occur in play environments.

4 State two situations in which you can deal with a hazard your self; and two situations where the hazard must be reported to someone else.

5 Explain the types of information about health, safety and welfare that children and young people will need for a play opportunity, and how to give such information effectively.

6 Describe how you should judge the level of supervision to give during play opportunities according to the type of opportunity, the environment and the ages, stages of development and needs of the children.

Deal with accidents and emergencies

Unit C35

Safety in the play setting is an important part of a playworker's responsibility. Children and young people will from time to time have accidents. These may be minor accidents, such as colliding when running around, or more serious accidents, such as fractures. As a playworker, you therefore need to be able to act promptly, calmly and correctly in any situations and emergencies that arise.

This unit is divided into two elements:
- C35.1 Deal with injuries and signs of illness.
- C35.2 Follow emergency procedures.

The Play Value covered in this unit is shown below:

Value No	Statement
11	Play opportunities should be provided within the current legislative framework.

Element C35.1 Deal with injuries and signs of illness

What you need to learn
- How to identify and deal with accidents and illnesses.
- How to protect the casualty in an emergency situation.
- Setting procedures and your responsibility for reporting and recording.

How to identify and deal with accidents and illnesses

Within your setting, you may from time to time deal with children or young people who have either had a minor accident or feel unwell.

The types of minor accidents you may come across include:
- paper cuts
- bumped head
- grazes to knees, hands or elbows
- insect stings
- nose bleeds
- trapped fingers
- sprained ankles.

You may be required to treat any of these minor injuries, and the following table explains what to look out for and how to treat some of the more common injuries.

Injury	How to treat	Things to look out for
Friction burn	Rinse wound in cold running water.	Sore abrasions, e.g. elbow and knees.
Graze	Rinse wound with cold water. Allow to heal in the air.	Sore abrasions, e.g. elbow and knees.
Bump to the head	Apply cold compress, e.g. a bag of frozen peas, a bruise soother or a wet hand towel.	Drowsiness, pale skin, vomiting, headaches, nosebleeds. This is serious, so seek medical attention especially if the blood appears thin and watery, as it could be a sign that cerebrospinal fluid is leaking from the brain.
Nose bleed	Tip the head forward, pinch the soft part of the nose just below the bridge, apply wrapped crushed ice to the area.	Seek medical attention if the bleeding continues for more than 20 minutes, or if it is mixed with clear fluids.
Insect stings	Reassure the casualty, use a wrapped ice pack to reduce the swelling.	Seek urgent medical help if the child is starting to look ill or is having trouble breathing because this could indicate an allergic reaction.

The types of illness you may come across as a playworker include:

- common cold
- influenza (flu)
- headache and migraine
- ear infections
- chicken pox, measles and mumps
- tonsillitis
- meningitis (you will need to seek emergency treatment for a child with this illness)
- sickness
- stomach ache.

Children may display behavioural signs and/or physical signs to show that they are feeling unwell, as shown in the diagram overleaf.

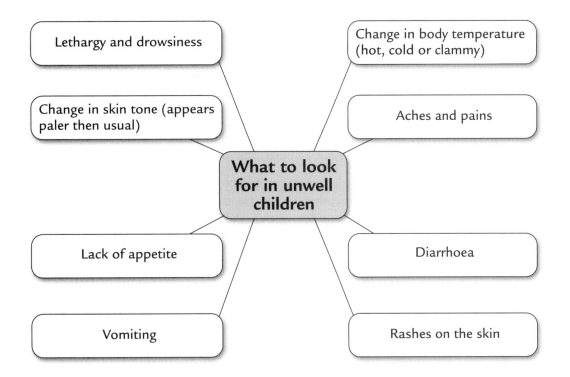

Illnesses vary in severity, and it is important to gather information on individual children or young people to enable you to assess the severity of each illness. The table below gives examples of how to recognise some illnesses.

Illness	How to recognise it
Common cold/flu	Sore throat, runny nose, high temperature, irritability
Sore throat/tonsillitis	Difficulty in swallowing, sore throat, aches and pains, headache, rise in body temperature
Heatstroke	Headache, dizziness, discomfort, restlessness, hot flushed skin
Gastro-enteritis	Nausea, vomiting, diarrhoea, dehydration
Chicken pox	Group of red spots with white centres that become itchy, change in body temperature
Measles	Rise in body temperature, runny eyes, cough, red blotchy rash
Meningitis	Headache, fever, confusion, dislike of light, small red spots beneath the skin that do not disappear when a glass is pressed against them

The actions to take when a child feels unwell are:

- make the child comfortable
- ensure that the child is not too hot or cold; fetch a blanket or coat if the child is feeling cold
- offer a drink (water), and isolate if necessary
- contact the parents or carers; use the emergency contact forms
- record the incident in the incident log (this may be in your accident book)
- in the event of a serious illness, call the **emergency services**.

If you have children or young people in your setting with medical conditions, for example diabetes or epilepsy, you should have details of the specific condition for each person and how to deal with it should symptoms arise. Medical conditions vary and individual records need updating and checking on a regular basis.

As a playworker, it may be your role to deal with any of the above. If you experience a more serious injury or illness, your role will be to call emergency services. It is therefore important that your respond appropriately following the guidelines of your setting.

If a child has an accident or is not feeling well you may be required to give support. This could be in the form of:

- monitoring the child or young person's condition, so you are able to pass on as much detailed information as possible to the qualified first aider
- staying with the **casualty**, to help reduce his or her anxiety
- looking at and talking to the casualty so he or she feels part of the situation
- staying calm and confident so the casualty feels more secure.

How to protect the casualty in an emergency situation

The first thing to understand is what is meant by a casualty. A casualty is a child, young person or adult who is injured or feels unwell and requires medical attention.

Sometimes you may have a casualty with a particular need. This can be either a medical or physical condition, such as a hearing or sight impairment, Downs Syndrome or a food allergy, and the casualty may need special attention following an accident or **emergency**. These details will be included on the individual's personal records.

On discovery of a casualty, you will need to assess the situation in a calm and controlled manner and assess the casualty's needs. It is important to protect yourself, as you do not want to become a casualty too.

In an emergency situation:

- stay calm, take a moment to think, do not put yourself in danger
- use your common sense, think about other, similar situations you have been in
- do not attempt too much alone, send for or call someone to help
- be aware of potential dangers, such as further injuries or injuries to others
- look for clues as to what caused the situation, e.g. glass, electrical fault, slippery floor, etc.

Think about it

Imagine you are visiting a local nature reserve and come across a child or young person in difficulty in the water. You cannot swim, but nearby is small rowing boat, a life buoy (fluorescent plastic ring that can be used to help rescue a casualty in water) and a sign of what to do in an emergency.

What action would you take?

In an emergency situation, you must put your safety first – you cannot help others if you become a casualty. Be aware of your limitations. Remember, you are not a medical practitioner and you may only have one other worker with you. Decide whether to contact the on-site first aider or to call the emergency services by assessing the situation. An example of the action you should take in an emergency situation is given below.

You are in the outside play area and a 9-year-old boy falls off a skateboard and breaks his leg.

1 Assess the situation.

↓

2 Make the area safe.

↓

3 Remove the audience.

↓

4 Do not move the casualty.

↓

5 Calm and reassure the casualty.

↓

6 Ask what hurts and if he can feel anything.

↓

7 Send someone to call an ambulance and contact the parents or carer using the Child Registration forms.

↓

8 Stay with the casualty.

↓

9 Keep him warm and reassure him.

↓

10 Do not give him anything to eat or drink.

↓

11 When the ambulance arrives pass on any details available.

↓

12 If possible, a member of staff should go with the child.

↓

13 Complete the accident report form/book.

It is important to provide comfort and reassurance to the casualty and others involved. This will reduce any anxiety the casualty may feel and prevent panic among bystanders. You should provide any treatment the casualty requires. Remember that you will have built up a good relationship with the children and they will look to you for reassurance. Below is a table of the types of reassurance you could give to a casualty and any other children or young people involved.

Casualty reassurance	Bystander reassurance
Talk quietly. Reassure him or her. Hold the casualty's hand to comfort him or her. Do not panic, remain calm. Distract the casualty by talking about something that interests him or her. Give him or her a cuddle. Stay with the casualty. Explain what is happening so the casualty is fully aware of what is happening to him or her.	Remove them from the immediate area (to avoid endangering others, upsetting the casualty further by having an audience, and so that treatment can be given efficiently). Provide a calm atmosphere. Explain what is happening. Occupy bystanders to prevent them from panicking or saying things that might upset the casualty further. Listen and offer reassurance.

CASE STUDY

Shameen and Leah are skipping in the outside area. Shameen trips over her rope, falling to the floor. She is lying on the ground crying holding her knee. You go over and see that she has badly grazed her knee.

1 What would you do?
2 What records would you need to complete?

In order to be more confident with dealing with emergency situations, it is recommended that you undertake a first aid course. If you come across a casualty with any of the symptoms described in the spider diagram below, and a person who can offer **qualified assistance** is not on site, you must call the emergency services. They will give you advice and instructions about what to do.

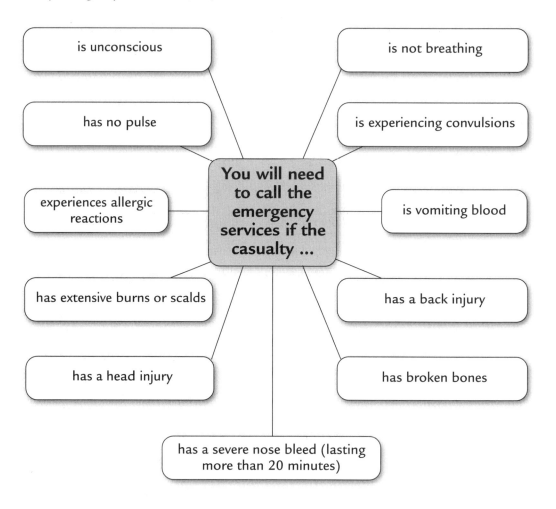

If you need to contact the emergency services, you will be required to give the operator as much information as possible. The operator will ask you certain questions to ascertain the degree of the emergency.

Setting procedures and your responsibility for reporting and recording

Whatever the illness or injury, the procedures and policies of your setting should be followed. The guidance given in the National Standards is shown overleaf.

Standard 7: First aid

- There is a first aid box complying with the Health and Safety (First Aid) Regulations (1981), the contents of which should be checked frequently and replaced as necessary by a designated member of staff. It is kept in an accessible place out of reach of children.
- There is at least one member of staff with a current first aid certificate on the premises or on outings at any one time. The first aid qualification includes training in first aid for infants and young children.
- Written parental permission is requested, at the time of the placement, to seek any necessary emergency medical advice or treatment in the future.
- A record is maintained, signed by the parent, of any accidents.

ACTIVE KNOWLEDGE

Find out the following information:

- who your on-site first aider is and how to contact them
- where the children's details are kept for contacting parents or carers in an emergency
- the correct emergency procedures you should follow in your setting when contacting the emergency services
- where the telephone is located and how to use it
- where the first aid box is located.

All types of accidents must be reported to parents and logged in the accident book. This is a legal requirement and conforms with the Health and Safety Act (1974). When recording the accident it is important to include all **other information** and information about **other people involved**. Parents may be given a letter, which tells them what happened and how their child was treated. To the right is an example of a letter a child may take home; overleaf is an example of a page out of an accident book.

Calverton out-of-school club

Dear Parent/Carer   Date: *14 March*

Your child _____ *Joe* _____ had a bump on the head while at the setting today.

If you notice any of the following symptoms, please contact your doctor:

- your child vomits
- your child complains of a headache
- your child behaves differently.

Yours sincerely

Name	Date	Time	Accident/ incident	Treatment	Treated or witnessed by	Parent, guardian or person with parental responsibility
Joe Bloggs	14.4.03	5 pm	Fell off climbing frame, cut lip and banged his head (right side)	Cold compress, TLC	Playworker: Jane Smith	Mrs Bloggs

An accident book

Every setting should have at least one first aid kit. There is no mandatory ruling of the items that should be in a kit because this will depend on the size of setting, the number of employees and the nature of work, etc. As a guide, the minimum stock in a first aid kit would consist of the following:

- 20 individually wrapped sterile adhesive dressings (assorted sizes)
- 2 sterile eye pads
- 4 individually wrapped triangular bandages
- 6 safety pins
- 6 medium sterile unmedicated wound dressings (approximately 12 cm × 12 cm)
- 2 large sterile unmedicated wound dressings (approximately 18 cm × 18 cm)
- 1 pair of disposable gloves.

Contents of the kit should be checked regularly and stock replenished soon after it has been used. Expiry dates should be checked, such as those on sterile water bottles, and items should not be used after that date. Most settings have a monitoring book to show who checked the kit, when, and what was added.

Every setting will have records of how to contact parents in an emergency. Parents provide this information when their child first joins the setting. Emergency contact information should be checked regularly and updated if necessary by a designated member of staff such as a supervisor. An example of the information required is shown opposite.

Child's name _____

Address _____

Telephone number _____

Emergency contact (1)

Name _____

Address _____

Telephone number _____

Emergency contact (2)

Name _____

Address _____

Telephone number _____

✓ ACTIVE KNOWLEDGE

Find out the following information:
- where accidents are recorded in your setting
- what details you need to record
- where personal information and records are kept
- what the policy is with regard to updating emergency contact information
- how parents are informed in an emergency.

There are clear guidelines on giving medicine to children and young people (see Standard 7). Some settings will not give medicine, while others do as long as the child or young person is not contagious.

Standard 7: Administering medicine

- Medicine is stored in its original container, clearly labelled and inaccessible to children.
- Medicines are not usually administered unless they have been prescribed for that child by a doctor.
- The parent gives prior written permission to administer medication.
- Written records are kept of all medicines administered to children, and parents sign the record book to acknowledge the entry.
- If the administration of prescription medicines requires technical/medical knowledge, then individual training is provided for staff from a qualified health professional. Training is specific to the individual child concerned.

The policies and procedures of your setting are there to give you and the parents or carers guidance, and your role is to implement these at all times. Below is an example of a policy, with regard to sick children in your care.

Calverton out-of-school club sick children policy

The club will inform OfSTED of any infectious disease that a qualified medical person considers notifiable. The club and staff will also recognise and act to:

- protect the rights of the individual with regards to equality, access and opportunity
- follow medical advice and the procedures related to infectious, notifiable and communicable diseases
- care for the sick child while awaiting collection
- be aware of the implications for other children and staff
- make this policy available to staff
- inform parents of occurrences and reoccurrences of infection
- regularly update emergency contact numbers and the children's medical details
- make contingency arrangements when parents cannot be contacted or cannot collect a sick child
- keep abreast of current local health issues.

Parents are asked to keep their children at home if they have an infection and to inform the club as to the nature of the infection, so that the club can alert other parents.

The club will make careful observations of any child who seems unwell. Parents are asked not to bring into the club any child who has been vomiting or had diarrhoea until at least 48 hours have elapsed after cessation of symptoms.

ACTIVE KNOWLEDGE

1 Ask your senior playworker if there are any children with medical conditions that you should be aware of.
2 How would you deal with the following situations?

- During an outdoor game of football, Delroy is tackled from behind and falls to the ground. He holds his knee and groans loudly.
- During a video session, you notice that Chloe has gone quiet. Before you have time to do anything, she begins to vomit.

CONSOLIDATION

Think of a time when you have dealt with the following situations at your setting:

- an accident
- a child or a young person showing signs of illness.

Recall and record these incidents. Remember to explain your role in the situation, say what you did and why you did it, and relate your actions to theory.

What you need to learn

- The procedures of your setting for dealing with emergencies.
- Evacuation procedures.
- The reporting procedure.

The procedures of your setting for dealing with emergencies

In your role as a playworker, you may have to deal with different emergencies such as fire, security incidents, floods, electrical faults or any other situation which threatens the health and safety of children, young people, staff and yourself. You may be required to lead an evacuation of the building. There should be a written policy available at your setting regarding such emergencies; make sure you are aware of it and have read it. Examples of emergency procedures are given on pages 109–10.

Fire

In the event of a fire:

1 Raise the alarm (blow the whistle, sound the fire alarm, ring the bell).

2 Instruct everyone to leave the building quickly from a safe exit. The fire exits should have clear signs and be unobstructed at all times. There should be notices displayed explaining the procedures.

3 Assemble at a safe place away from the building, possibly a play area, keeping away from the access point.

4 Take the register to check that all children, young people and adults are present.

5 Do not re-enter the building for any reason until the safety officer gives you permission to do so.

Security incidents

If you have a stranger or intruder on site:

1 Observe the person's behaviour (in a school setting it could be a parent waiting to collect their child from an after-school activity).
2 If you are uneasy about the person's presence, move the children or young people away from the area, e.g. return to the building.
3 Notify your senior worker, who may approach the stranger.
4 If the stranger is causing concern and will not leave the site, telephone the police for assistance. Give the police a description of the person's appearance and behaviour.

Missing persons

On finding that you have a child or young person missing from your care, you should carry out the following procedures:

1 Ask staff and children or young people if they have seen the **missing person** and where this last was.
2 Gather the group together in a safe place while a member of staff searches the setting and grounds.
3 If the child or young person is not found, contact his or her parents or carers. If the child or young person is not with the parents, contact the local police. Give a description of the child or young person, i.e. clothing, general appearance. Emergency contact details for each child or young person should be in the registration documents for that individual.

✓ ACTIVE KNOWLEDGE

1 In the event of a fire:
- What should you do when you hear the fire alarm?
- Why should fire exits be kept unobstructed?
- Why do you need to take the register?
- When is it safe to re-enter the building?

2 In the event of a security alert:
- Why should you not automatically assume the stranger is a danger to the children in your care?
- Who could you notify of your concerns?
- What information do you need to give to the police?

3 If a person goes missing:
- Why should you ask the children and your colleagues if they have seen the missing person?
- Why doesn't all of the group go looking for the missing person?
- Who could you report a missing person to?
- What information would you need to give when reporting a missing person?

Evacuation procedures

Your setting is required by law to have evacuation procedures on display. These are normally in prominent positions, e.g. by the door or window, and will probably be similar to the one shown below.

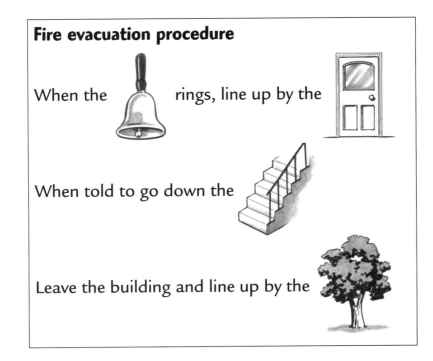

Fire evacuation procedure

When the [bell] rings, line up by the [door]

When told to go down the [stairs]

Leave the building and line up by the [tree]

Keys to good practice: Evacuating the building

✓ Do not stop to collect personal belongings.
✓ Stay calm.
✓ Ensure everyone has left the building.
✓ Do not use the lift.
✓ Close doors behind you.
✓ Take the register with you.

CASE STUDY

Bénace, who has a hearing impairment, is helping you to make the sandwiches. The fire alarm goes off.

1 What would you do and why?

Most places practise a fire drill to check that the evacuation system works well but nevertheless, problems such as those shown below may occur.

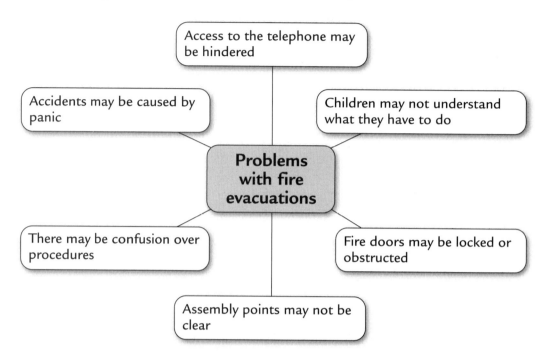

If any of these problems occur during a fire drill, it is vital to keep a record of the problems and to report them to senior colleagues, in order to:

- avoid recurrence
- ensure correct procedures are carried out
- meet legal requirements
- protect yourself.

The reporting procedure

A record is required of the drills that are carried out each term. The example below shows the type of information held on a fire evacuation drill form.

Evaluation form (fire drill)

Date of drill: Friday 16 May

Time evacuation took: 2 minutes 25 seconds

Number of children present: 20

Number of adults present: 3

Comments on how the drill went: The drill went well, all were aware of the procedures

---

ACTIVE KNOWLEDGE

1 Ensure that you know the policy of your setting for:
- contacting the emergency services
- the location of emergency services numbers
- parents and carers emergency telephone numbers.

2 Find out the following:
- how often children's records are updated at your setting and whether they include a description of the child or young person
- what your role would be during an evacuation of the building.

3 How would you deal with the following situations:
- **a** During an evening session, a child approaches you and informs you that the socket the play station is plugged into is sizzling and there is smoke coming from the plug.
- **b** The door at your setting has been left open on a hot sunny day. You hear a commotion in the corner of the room and you notice that there is a swarm of bees in the room.
- **c** During a fire drill you identify the following areas of concern:
  - you and your colleague both checked the toilet
  - one child fell over a chair that was obstructing the exit
  - two children had gone home and this had not been marked on the register.

CONSOLIDATION

Recall a time when you have been involved in emergency procedures. Write a reflective account of this, remembering to include your own role in the situation and to evaluate the process.

END OF UNIT TEST

1 List the types of injuries and illnesses that may occur in your area of work.

2 Explain why it is important to provide comfort and reassurance to someone in an emergency situation, and how to do so.

3 Describe the emergency procedures in your place of work for fires, security incidents and missing persons.

4 State the types of problems that may occur when you are carrying out emergency procedures, why you should report them and who you should report them to.

Support the protection of children from abuse

In the role of a playworker, you may have children and young people in your care who are particularly vulnerable and in need of help and protection from possible abuse. It is important that you are able to recognise the signs and symptoms of suspected abuse, that you know how to respond to these children and young people in a helpful way, and that you know the correct action to take in these circumstances.

This whole area is known as child protection. In matters of child protection, you will need to be aware of and follow the policies and procedures of your setting, which will have been written to meet the legal requirements. Playworkers involved in child protection issues will need to remember that the safety and security of the child or young person is of paramount importance.

It may be that, in your role, you never encounter child abuse, but it is still important to know what to do so that you can respond correctly and immediately. Being involved in a child protection issue can be a very traumatic experience, and because of the delicacy of the situation you will need to be aware of who to discuss it with and who to turn to for help and support.

This unit is divided into two elements:
- C36.1 Report signs of possible abuse.
- C36.2 Respond to a child's **disclosure of abuse**.

The Play Values covered in this unit are shown below:

Value No	Statement
1	The child must be at the centre of the process.
4	An environment must be provided that stimulates and provides opportunities for risks and challenges, and growth of confidence and self-esteem.
5	A play environment must be provided in which children feel physically and personally safe and able to take part in activities free from hazards.
6	Every child is an individual and should be respected for who they are.
7	As playworker, you should be considerate and caring.
8	As playworker, you should promote equal opportunities for all children and young people in your setting, regardless of ability, race, culture, social background, etc.

Children and young people should be free to enjoy life and be given the opportunity to reach their full potential. They should be able to do this without fear or physical discomfort. Anything that gets in the way of this needs investigating.

Although there are many kinds of abuse, for children we concentrate on four main types:

- neglect
- physical abuse
- emotional abuse
- sexual abuse.

The ability to identify signs that might indicate abuse is part of a playworker's role.

Neglect is when carers fail to meet the basic needs of the children and young people in their care. It causes damage to health, safety and wellbeing. Neglect can be physical, emotional or intellectual, and can include leaving children unsupervised, not providing suitable food and clothing, as well as refusing to give adequate love and affection to children.

Physical abuse is when a child or young person has been deliberately hurt or injured, or when someone has failed to prevent physical injury and/or suffering. It could be extreme physical punishment, deliberate suffocation, poisoning or deliberate non-accidental physical injury, such as hitting a child with a belt.

Emotional abuse affects a child or young person's wellbeing and development, and can be suffered either emotionally or psychologically. It involves emotional ill treatment, such as constantly ignoring children. These children and young people often lack love, security and the company of friendly people.

Sexual abuse covers a range of sexual activities that children and young people are encouraged to, or forced to, endure and/or watch. It includes sexual activity which is unlawful and to which the child is unable to give informed consent. It can involve looking at pornographic material, sexual intercourse and/or inappropriate touching.

✓ ACTIVE KNOWLEDGE

Look at the instances below and decide which type of abuse you may suspect.

1 A child bends down to tie his shoelace and his shirt rides up; you notice little round burns on his lower back.
2 The weather turns very cold and it snows for five days. Each day Jane comes to the setting in sandals (with no socks), a thin shirt and skirt, and no coat.
3 During a swimming session you see red suction marks on a 12-year-old girl's thigh and lower neck.

The Children Act (1989) sets out legal responsibilities regarding the protection of children. The main message from the Act is that the child's welfare (their wellbeing) must always come first. This means that your first concern as a playworker must be the child or young person. Parents and carers have rights, but they also have responsibilities and the Children Act explains these. One responsibility is to keep their children safe and secure from personal harm.

In all child protection investigations, the Children Act states that:

- the child must be consulted about any decisions that are made
- wherever possible, the child or young person should stay within their family (unless this would put the child in danger)
- parental responsibility must be taken into consideration
- all investigations must follow the assessment framework guidelines.

Each local authority has an Area Child Protection Committee (ACPC). This committee must follow set guidelines called the Child Protection Framework. The framework is designed to ensure that the local authorities follow the directives of the Children Act by responding to suspected abuse in a consistent manner and within a set timescale. The framework guidelines ensure that the approach focuses on the wellbeing of the child by taking into account all aspects of the child or young person's life. This is called a holistic approach. At all times, the child must be at the centre of the process and the most important thing is to safeguard the child and promote his or her welfare. The three main areas (domains) in the holistic approach are:

- parenting capacity
- the child's developmental needs
- family and environmental factors.

Each domain is divided into smaller parts, rather like the elements in each of the NVQ units.

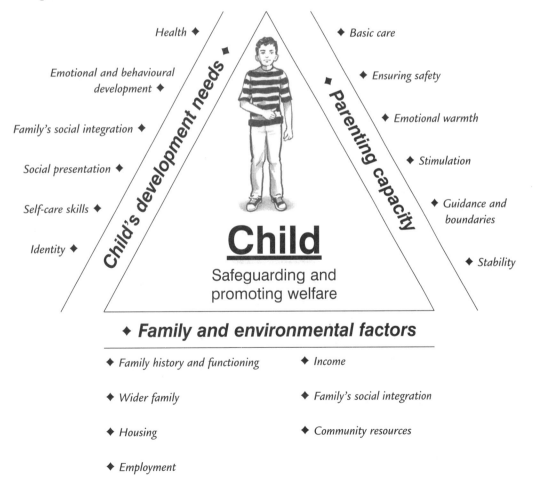

Each setting will have policies and procedures that a playworker must follow if abuse is suspected, and these policies will be in line with the National Standards set by the DfES (see below).

Standard 13: Suspected abuse

The registered person complies with local child protection procedures approved by the Area Child Protection Committee and ensures that all adults working and looking after children in the provision are able to put the procedures into practice.

- The protection of the child is the registered person's first priority.
- The registered person has a written statement, based on the Area Child Protection Committee procedures, clearly stating staff responsibilities with regard to reporting of suspected child abuse or neglect and including contact names and telephone numbers. It includes procedures to be followed in the event of an allegation being made against a member of staff or volunteer. These procedures are shared with parents before admission to the day care.
- The registered person ensures that all staff are aware of possible symptoms of children at risk and their responsibility to report concerns according to Area Child Protection Committee procedures without delay and to keep concerns confidential.

The policies of your setting will have a section on child protection. The policy will usually start with a general statement (as shown below) and then include several sections.

Calverton out-of-school club child protection policy

We intend to create in our club an environment in which children are safe from abuse and in which any suspicion of abuse is promptly and appropriately responded to.

Examples of the types of sections that could be included in your setting's policy include:

- The exclusion of known abusers. This section will state the conditions and requirements for all workers (paid and voluntary) and will state that all workers will be checked with the Criminal Records Bureau.
- If a child arrives with injuries, the setting's procedure to deal with this.
- Responding appropriately to suspicion of abuse. This section will explain how the setting will respond and who will be informed.
- The records that will need to be completed and kept.
- How to liaise with other agencies and bodies who will become involved, e.g. Social Services, NSPCC.
- Supporting the family – the position of the staff and club in supporting and working with the family.

✓ **ACTIVE KNOWLEDGE**

Look at your setting's policies to check:
- who the designated member of staff for child protection is
- what you should do if you suspect abuse.

As a playworker, you will have a set course of action to take if you suspect that a child or young person in your care is in danger of being abused. When you first started your job, the guidelines for this course of action should have been explained and given to you to read. You may have a flow chart, similar to the one below, that shows exactly what your role is.

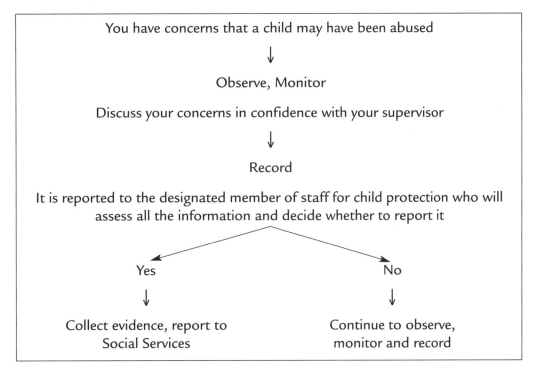

You have concerns that a child may have been abused

↓

Observe, Monitor

Discuss your concerns in confidence with your supervisor

↓

Record

It is reported to the designated member of staff for child protection who will assess all the information and decide whether to report it

Yes → Collect evidence, report to Social Services

No → Continue to observe, monitor and record

In some cases, abuse is hard to detect and confirm, so it is better to seek advice and share concerns with a relevant person – that way, you will have done something about it. It is far better to share concerns and find that you were wrong, than to ignore concerns and the child or young person come to harm.

It is important that, as a professional person, you follow your setting's guidelines and respect confidentiality. This means that you need to be careful who you discuss your concerns with, where you discuss them and where you keep your notes and records. If you do not observe confidentiality and information is leaked out, you could find yourself faced with all kinds of legal problems. Your job will be in jeopardy and the reputation of the setting will have been damaged.

All records will need to be kept in a locked cabinet, and may not be available to all of the staff; only people directly concerned with the situation need access to them, e.g. the child's key worker, the setting supervisor or a designated member of staff. The parents of the child concerned have a right to see the records if they ask to.

What you need to learn

- The common signs and indicators of abuse.
- Recognising abuse.
- Other types of information to consider.
- Sensitive observation of children.
- The importance of recording signs of abuse.

The common signs and indicators of abuse

Before you can report any signs of possible abuse, you need to understand the different types of abuse and be able to recognise and identify indicators of suspected abuse. As a playworker, you will have regular contact with the children and young people in your care so will be in a valuable position when it comes to noticing physical, emotional and behavioural changes. It is a sad fact that some children are abused sometimes by the people who are supposed to love and care for them, e.g. parents and family. Identifying abuse can be difficult and it is important to look at all contributing factors, not just the physical signs.

Physical abuse

Physical abuse can be wide ranging, as shown below.

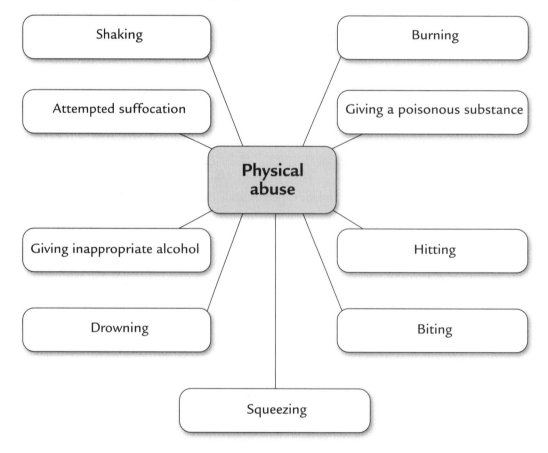

As soon as you recognise any physical injuries you will be required to report these. This may involve the use of a body map. This is a picture of a body on which you draw the injuries that you have observed. The injury in the diagram below shows a diagonal mark across the back. The pattern it has left indicates the type of object that possibly caused it was 2–3 inches wide; it could have been a belt.

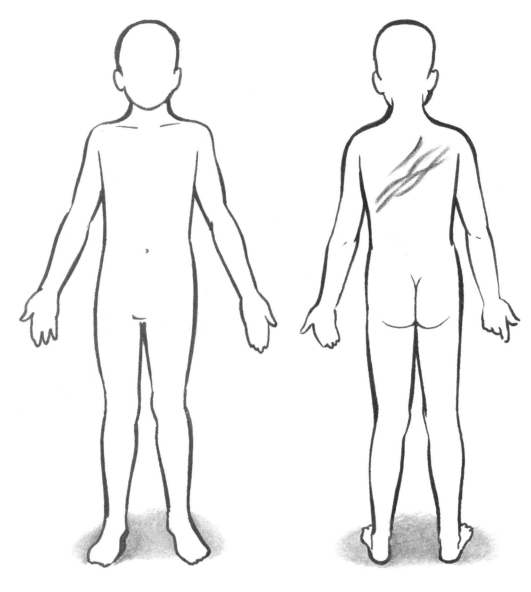

Front   Back

ACTIVE KNOWLEDGE

Six sets of injuries are shown below. See if you can identify the possible causes.

1

2

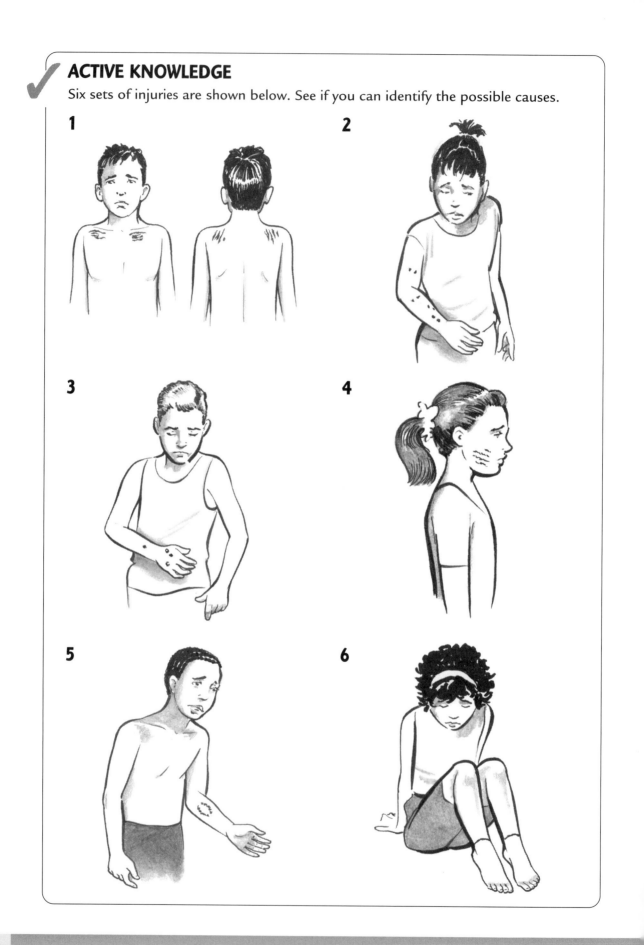

3

4

5

6

It is important to remember that potential signs and indicators of abuse need to be examined in a wider context before abuse can be diagnosed. Just because a child has a bruise, it does not mean that they have been abused – they may have fallen over or bumped into something. You should also take into account the explanation offered by the child or young person and see if that is consistent (matches) the injury or not. There are common sites on the body where accidental injuries normally occur, which are shown in the diagram below.

Common sites for <u>accidental</u> injury

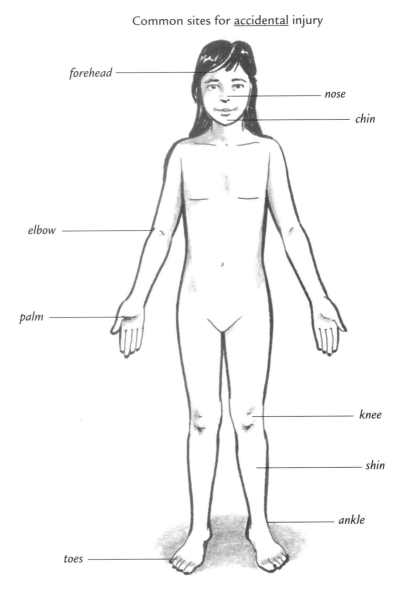

Accidental injuries are usually explained easily and have often been treated, e.g. a grazed knee. Even if the sign of injury is in the genital area, this may be due to an infection or constant wetness (e.g. the child not drying themselves properly) or irritation (e.g. from a bubble bath). Again, if accidental, this injury will most likely have been treated.

The common sites on the body where non-accidental injuries normally occur are shown on the diagram below.

Common sites for <u>non-accidental</u> injury

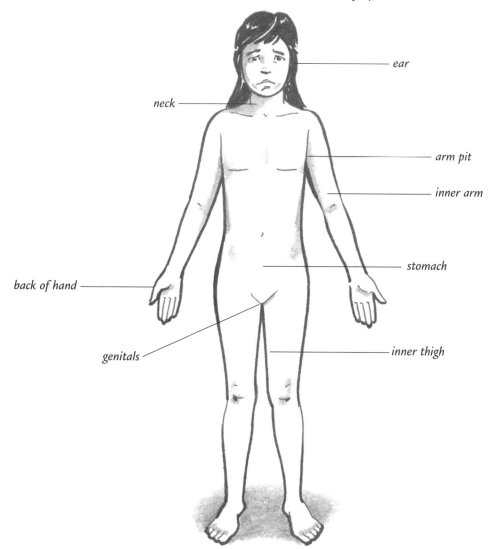

ear

neck

arm pit

inner arm

back of hand

stomach

genitals

inner thigh

🔑 **Keys to good practice: Suspecting non-accidental injury has occurred**

✓ Injuries are likely to be made on purpose by biting, scratching or cutting, and are often in the shape of the object that caused them.
✓ Injuries are often deep and untreated.
✓ X-rays show unreported fractures.
✓ There is a delay in seeking treatment.

Injury	Non-accidental injury – things to look out for
Bruises	Frequent and patterned, showing how they were made, e.g. finger/thumb marks, belt marks. They will appear in different colours as age will vary; it is unlikely they were all caused together.
Burns	Likely to form a pattern with a clear outline to show what caused them, e.g. cigarette, iron. They may appear in unusual positions, e.g. back of knees.
Genital	Soreness or bleeding around the genital area is a sign of a sexually transmitted disease. Bite and scratch marks may also be visible.
Fractures	Likely to be numerous and may be healing at different rates.

Think about it

Read the two scenarios below and then think about how to explain them.

1 Kyle is 7 years old. He shows you a mark on his upper arm. It is on the outside and it is about 1 centimetre in diameter. You think it looks like a burn mark from a cigarette. He says that he walked into his mum's cigarette after he had had his bath the previous evening.

2 Ben took his shoes off when he and his friends built a den in one corner of the room. He is putting them back on so he can go outside to play football. As he pulls his foot up to tie the lace you see three round marks (about 1 centimetre in diameter) near his sock line. They look like cigarette burns. You casually ask him what he has done to his legs, he says nothing, then changes his mind and says he caught his leg on the bunk bed at home.

Compare the two scenarios above, both marks look like cigarette burns. Think:

- In which example is the child telling the truth?
- How could you check this out?
- Who would you discuss it with?
- What would you record?

On the surface, the first example looks more likely to have been an accident in the home; the position of the mark and the explanation seem to tally. Once it has been checked out with the parent you may find that your initial reactions were correct. You should still record the incident (and date it) with a brief explanation, just in case the same thing happens again. If the parent gives another explanation that does not seem feasible, you should share your concerns, once more recording the details.

The second example immediately seems more suspicious and your concerns should be shared. Remember not to press the child for too many details, you just need enough to be able to convince yourself that this is a case to be referred for possible abuse. People far more experienced and trained will be interviewing and discussing the injury with the child in more detail at a later date. Your responsibility is the passing on of concerns to the designated member of staff for child protection.

Children and young people who have been physically abused often undergo behaviour changes. These could include:

- unusually withdrawn or aggressive behaviour, e.g. suddenly not wanting to join in activities, sitting alone, becoming violent quickly in arguments
- cowering to sudden movements, e.g. if you were to pass them something they would flinch
- violence in role-play situations, e.g. they take on an authoritarian role and may shout and threaten other children playing with them
- aggression towards children and young people, e.g. hitting, biting, pushing to get their own way
- shying from physical contact, e.g. if you sit close to them they will move their chair away from you
- lack of trust, e.g. constantly checking things out.

The explanations and attitude of the parent or carer can also lead you to suspect abuse, for example if they:

- blame someone else
- do not show remorse, concern or guilt
- blame the child for the injury
- justify the injury by saying the child deserves it
- deny anything is wrong.

As a playworker it may not be part of your role, according to the child protection procedures of your setting, to talk to the parents. This will probably be the role of the designated member of staff. However, it is useful to be aware of the types of parental behaviour that could be seen as suspicious.

Keys to good practice: Suspecting physical abuse

✓ When you suspect abuse you need to look at all the details and take a holistic view of the child or young person. Not all the behavioural signs and parental responses will confirm that the child has been abused.

✓ In matters of possible abuse it is important not to jump to conclusions. For example, just because a child has a burn mark on his arm it does not automatically mean that he or she has been abused; it could have been an accident.

Sexual abuse

A range of indicators may lead you to suspect a child is a victim of sexual abuse. Some indicators may be outwardly observable, while others may be sensed intuitively. Examples of **physical and behavioural signs and indicators of abuse** are shown in the table below.

Possible physical indicators	Possible behavioural indicators
Itchiness or discomfort in the genital or anal area	Excessive preoccupation with sex, always referring to sexual issues
Sexually transmitted diseases	Eating or sleeping problems
Blood stains on underwear	Excessive masturbation
Bruises or scratches on genitalia, anus or buttocks	Sexual knowledge above their developmental level
Bite marks on thighs	Not wanting to be with certain people
Abnormal swellings	Over-sexual behaviour that is not appropriate to age or development level
Frequent visits to the toilet	
In girls: pregnancy, vaginal discharge	Knowledge and use of sexually explicit language beyond their age and stage of development
In boys: pain in urinating, penile discharge or swelling	Low self-esteem or lacking in self-confidence

In matters of possible abuse it is important not to jump to conclusions, for example, just because a child is visiting the toilet more than usual, this does not automatically mean that she has been abused. She may have drunk a lot or have an infection.

Neglect

You may suspect that children are being neglected when adults fail to meet the needs of children and young people in their care. Neglect includes failing to protect the child or young person, or to ensure his or her health, safety and wellbeing. Neglect can take many forms and can be:

- intellectual neglect, e.g. not talking and listening to a child
- emotional neglect, e.g. not giving a child love and attention
- physical neglect, e.g. not providing adequate clothing.

Neglect can also be one or a mixture of the following:

- deliberate, i.e. when a person knows what they are doing and why they are doing it, e.g. not providing clothes suitable for the weather
- unintentional, i.e. when a person is unaware that something should or should not be done, e.g. a parent with learning difficulties or poor parenting skills; it may be that the parent is not able to read the letter from school about a packed lunch and so will not send one for their child
- unavoidable, i.e. when it is difficult to stop it, e.g. a parent with physical difficulties or health problems; it could be a single parent who needs to be on a dialysis machine for four hours a day and so cannot adequately supervise her children.

Examples of suspected neglect are shown in the table below.

Example	Indicator
Children not given a balanced nutritious diet	They are often hungry or eat only crisps and chips
Children lack medical care	They often have untreated illnesses and injuries
Children live in unhygienic conditions	They often have dirty clothes and body odour
Children do not have suitable clothing	They wear sandals in the snow and do not have a coat
Children are not kept from physical danger	They have repeated accidental injuries
Children have access to very little education	They have very few books and toys, their school attendance is poor
Children do not have enough exercise or rest	They are tired and lethargic

Emotional abuse

Just like neglect, children who are emotionally abused lack love, attention and guidance. They have little experience of friendly people to take an interest in them and care for them. This often means the child is unhappy and their development and wellbeing will be affected. Things to look out for when identifying emotional abuse include the following:

- children who have low self-esteem and low self-confidence; they think that they are not good at anything
- children who have behaviour difficulties; they are often challenging and attention seeking
- children who are abnormally passive or lethargic; they show little interest and do not want to join in activities
- children who have delayed social development; they may find it hard to share with other children
- children who have speech disorders, they may be unable to pronounce words and be understood
- children who have an inability to play and have fun; they may not use their imagination and so take on an observer role in play
- children who are very sensitive to parents' moods; if their mum arrives in a rush the child may get upset if they are not ready to leave
- children who have difficulties in making friends; they may play alone or stay with an adult
- children who display nervous behaviour; they may look anxious each time the door opens
- children who show poor concentration; they can stay on one task for only a short length of time
- children who display comfort seeking behaviour; they may always want to be near an adult.

Not all of the above indicators mean a child has been abused. Those who suffer emotional abuse are more likely to suffer other forms of abuse. Bullying can also be classed as emotional abuse, depending upon the form it takes.

Recognising abuse

It may be that during your time as a playworker you come to assess children and young people who you suspect are being abused. It may be an obvious physical sign or it may be signs of sexual or emotional abuse, which are sometimes harder to detect. The abuse may involve neglect or bullying. Whatever the form the suspected abuse takes, it is important to be aware of the correct procedures. Your first concerns will be for the child or young person, especially if they are in need of medical attention or in personal danger. You must in these circumstances act quickly. However, you may only have suspicions, in which case you will need to discuss your concerns and possibly observe and monitor the indicators until you have the required evidence to report the issue.

Think about it

Consider the scenarios below and think:
- What are the warning signs?
- Could there be another explanation?
- What action would you take?

1 Tyrone is 8 years old and he attends your after school club. Tyrone's mum goes out on Wednesdays and her friend's son, Dean, aged 18, baby-sits. Tyrone tells you that when Dean baby-sits he is allowed to stay up and watch Dean's videos. Dean has told Tyrone not to tell his mum or he will not let him stay up again.

2 Alfie is 9 years old and his sister is 6. They live with their mum in a two-bedroom flat. You overhear Alfie tell his friend that he is in charge at home now his mum has a cleaning job in an office. When you ask Alfie he tells you his mum works and he looks after his sister. He says it is OK because his mum locks the door.

3 Katie is 10 years old and lives with her mum. She visits and stays at her father's house along with her stepmother and stepbrothers on alternate weekends. You hear a conversation in which Katie asks a friend if they sleep in their underwear. She says that at the weekend the heating broke down and she and her stepbrothers all had to undress and share a bed, and they had to cuddle together to keep warm.

4 You set out an activity where the children are making passports. You ask the children to paint a picture of themselves. You notice Jade aged 10 has painted her self looking solemn and very unattractive. She tells you that she looks like this at home and that her father has told her she is fat and ugly like her mum.

Other types of information to consider

When a holistic view is taken of a child or young person you suspect is suffering from abuse, part of this process will look at other contributing factors. For example, has the child sustained an injury or several injuries that have been accidental through play, or are there other aspects of their circumstances and life to be taken into account? These factors may make a child or young person more vulnerable to abuse and are called predisposing factors. They are often caused by difficulties and stresses in an adult's life and their previous experiences. These factors may affect the attitude of the adult, making them less tolerant of the child or young person. Examples of such circumstances include:

- living in crowded conditions, e.g. a large family in a small flat
- your parenting skills; perhaps they did not have a positive role model in their own parents and so are unaware of the responsibilities of being a parent
- financial insecurity, surviving on very little money and unable to provide adequately for their children
- medication being taken for a medical condition or dependency
- social isolation, with no family or friends living near by to talk to and help them
- the use of physical punishment for control (this may have been their own experience and they are repeating this with their own family)
- a lack of love and attention; may be very unhappy and feel deserted and sad.

Sensitive observation of children

In your position as a playworker, you will have the opportunity to observe a child or young person's physical condition on many occasions, for example:

- when the children go swimming
- when they are changing for, or taking part in, sport activities
- during role-play and dressing up activities.

Whenever you observe a child's physical condition it should be done in a professional manner. You should be unobtrusive and discreet. This means that you are not obvious about what you are doing and you should not embarrass or draw attention to the fact that you are observing them.

Think about it

Decide which option you would take in the following situation.

A girl is playing a game of snakes and ladders with three other children and you notice a bruise on her inner arm that looks red and sore.

Option 1: You go over to the group and ask her, 'Who did that to your arm?'

Option 2: You wait until you are able to talk to her away from the other children and casually tell her that her arm looks sore and ask how she did it.

Keys to good practice: If you observe a sign of abuse

✓ Take the child or young person somewhere more private to talk to them (be careful not to put yourself at risk).
✓ Monitor and record your suspicions and actions.
✓ Use a body map to record the position of the injury.
✓ Follow the correct procedures of your setting.
✓ Inform your supervisor or designated member of staff.

The relationship that you as a playworker should develop and build with the children and young people in your care should be of a caring, friendly nature. It should be one where the children or young people feel valued, listened to and at ease to exchange ideas, opinions and information, but also one where they feel they can express their emotions and thoughts (positive and negative) freely to people who are understanding, caring and non-judgmental. It is vital that the children or young people feel comfortable and safe in the play setting. As a playworker, you can aid this process by:

- working closely with parents and carers
- providing a welcoming, friendly atmosphere
- being friendly, approachable and caring
- providing a range of play experiences where children and young people are able to express, show and deal with their emotions
- promoting personal safety for children in discussion and activities
- encouraging and praising the children to help them gain self-confidence and self-esteem.

Your setting should have clear policies on child protection that should be available and explained to parents and carers as well as workers. All workers in the setting should be aware of, and understand their role and responsibility in, implementing these policies.

The importance of recording signs of abuse

Each setting will have a set of charts and forms that will need completing when you suspect abuse. These will explain your role and what you should do if you suspect abuse. When you start your job or placement, you will be given the policies and procedures of the setting and you may be asked to sign to say you have read and understood them. You must use the correct paperwork to report signs of abuse. Your reports should be accurate, and you should distinguish between directly observed signs of abuse and other information from different sources. If giving an opinion you must indicate that it is an opinion. The things you need to record will include the following:

- date
- time
- child or young person's name
- parent's name
- place
- your name
- any witnesses.

In your report, you will need to describe exactly what you observed and did up to the stage where you passed the information and issue on to the designated member of staff. As a playworker, you may not have been involved in all the points mentioned below, but if you were, you will need to include them in your report:

- any physical signs (you could use a body map)
- any behavioural changes
- how the conversation or observation came about
- exactly what was said

- any explanation offered by the child and/or parents
- who you passed your concerns to.

All records should be kept confidential and should be locked securely away.

CONSOLIDATION

1 Think of an instance when you observed a child's physical condition and noticed an injury, e.g. a bruise, cut or graze. You may have asked the child or young person how this came about. It is most likely this was not an instance of suspected abuse. Record this for your evidence.

2 If you have been involved in any instances of suspected abuse, write about these but remember to observe confidentiality at all times; any records you have completed will need to be kept at your setting but you may show them to your assessor. Record your conversations and remember to explain your rationale (why you did what you did).

3 If you have not been involved in recognising abuse, read the following scenarios and explain what you would do in each situation.

- You are at a summer play scheme and it is a very hot day. During a break in a game of basketball, some of the young people are extremely hot. Ryan and Paul take off their polo shirts to cool down. They tell Tom to take his shirt off too. Tom refuses, saying he is not hot. Ryan tries to pull at Tom's shirt and you see a mark on his back; it is dark and red and stretches from his shoulder blade to past his waist. Tom is getting very cross and upset with Ryan and Paul so you suggest they all have a drink of orange. Ryan then stops pulling the shirt and they all sit down and have a drink.

- Joanne came in with her mum to visit the playscheme prior to her starting with you. Her mum seemed anxious at the time and had a list of questions to ask you (which she said her husband had told her to ask). Joanne started the scheme the following week. She was very quiet and hardly spoke to the other children, even though she goes to school with them. She spent a lot of time reading or watching the others play. When asked by a playworker if she would like to join in a craft activity and make a model, she said she was no good at drawing and she was not allowed to take things home because her father tells her off.
- Tyrone is 7 years old; he is very thin and underweight and gets tired quickly. He rarely has any new clothes and the ones he has are often dirty and stained. He does not seem to have money for the tuck shop and he always wants to do activities that involve food. Last week he was seen trying to eat the pasta and seeds put out for a collage activity.

Element C36.2   Respond to a child's disclosure of abuse

What you need to learn
- What is disclosure?
- How to respond to disclosure in a professional and appropriate manner.
- How to help children and young people protect themselves.

What is disclosure?

Disclosure means to expose or reveal. In matters of child protection, when a child or young person discloses this means that they have told you or given you clues that they have been or are the victim of some kind of abuse.

- Full disclosure is when a child or young person tells someone that they have experienced or are experiencing abuse.
- **Partial disclosure** is when a child or young person partly tells someone that they have or are experiencing abuse. It may be that they give you a hint or clues, or tell you part of the information only.

Think about it

Look at the examples below and decide if the disclosure is full or partial.
- A 12-year-old girl tells you she is pregnant and that her uncle is the father.
- A 7-year-old tells you that he is frightened of his stepfather and he hides in the cupboard from him.

Whatever the type of disclosure, it is a very brave thing to do. It may be that the child or young person has already tried to tell someone else about the abuse and has been ignored.

How to respond to disclosure in a professional and appropriate manner

You may, hopefully, never have a child disclose to you as a playworker. However, you must know how to handle this type of situation in case it does happen. A prompt, calm and sensitive approach will help the child or young person. By following the policies and procedure of your setting, you will be able to support the child or young person through this very difficult period.

A prompt response is required when a child or young person discloses; this means you need to act without delay. Disclosure needs to be dealt with promptly for the reasons shown below.

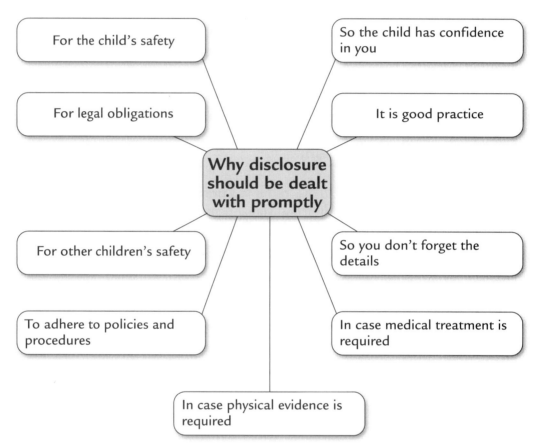

A prompt response will help ensure the child is put in no further danger.

By keeping calm, the playworker maintains a professional attitude, even though you may feel very anxious and even frightened for the child or young person. It will help ensure that the situation is not exacerbated (made worse) and it will help the child not to get unnecessarily upset. If you were to panic then this attitude may be passed on to the child or young person. By remaining calm, you will be able to be objective, think logically and pass on information clearly and accurately, exactly as your policies and procedures state. It is easy to make mistakes when you panic.

It is important to give support and reassurance to a child or young person who is about to disclose or who is in the process of disclosing. The effort involved in the child telling you is a tremendous thing for him or her. The child has to be extremely brave to even start to tell someone about things of this nature. As a caring adult, you need to show the child that telling you is the right thing and, by supporting the child, show you approve of what he or she has done and that you believe what he or she is saying. Support and reassurance will help to make disclosure as comfortable an experience as possible for the child, so they do not feel alone or afraid.

When a child begins to disclose, it will most likely be a time when you are working with them. In this instance, you will want to give the child or young person your full attention so you should, if possible, go somewhere private, but remember not to put yourself at risk. Remember to stay calm. Let the child or young person know that he or she did the right thing by telling you and that you believe him or her.

You should always let the child or young person set the pace of the conversation. By doing this, the child will feel more comfortable and more in control of the situation. The child may not tell everything if he or she feels pressurised. Listening carefully (active listening) will show that you are interested. Make sure that you give eye contact and make appropriate noises and responses to what the child says.

Remember that the child has chosen you to tell and this will mean that they feel comfortable in your presence and that they trust you to believe him or her and act in his or her own interest. You should not press for details or ask leading questions; the child or young person will be interviewed at a later stage by a professional and trained child protection specialist. You must ensure that you do not cross legal boundaries, e.g. do anything that may have a detrimental effect on future court proceedings. One thing that you must do, is explain to the child or young person that, for their own safety and wellbeing, you cannot keep what they tell you a secret.

It is your duty to inform others. This will include your supervisor and/or your designated member of staff for child protection. They will take up the case and deal with it according to set guidelines. By telling the child that you must inform others:

- the child is aware of the role you must take as a playworker
- the child will not feel betrayed when you do bring in other people
- you will build trust and respect, so the child knows that something will be done.

Because it is your legal obligation to tell others, you will need to explain to the child exactly who in the setting you need to inform. Explain that you and they will observe confidentiality and it will not be passed on to other children and their parents. By passing on information to the appropriate people, you are helping to prevent further abuse to the child or to other children within the family or locality who may be at risk.

Keys to good practice: Dealing with disclosure

✓ Be aware of whom to discuss issues with.

✓ Know how to maintain the confidentiality of the situation, and do not discuss it with anyone other than the designated person.

✓ Attend regular child protection training to renew and update your knowledge and understanding.

✓ Give the child or young person your full attention.

✓ If you can, go somewhere private where others cannot hear (remember not to put yourself at risk) .

✓ Stay calm.

✓ Let the child or young person set the pace of the conversation.

✓ Do not press for details or ask leading questions.

✓ Do not make promises you cannot keep.

✓ Use active listening techniques to listen carefully.

✓ Let the child or young person know that they did the right thing in telling you and that you believe him or her.

✓ Keep the child informed. Explain what you must do and why.

✓ Reassure the child that he or she is not to blame in any way for the abuse.

You will need to record disclosure accurately and promptly so that you do not forget or confuse the details of the conversation. It is important to remember the exact wording and terminology, so complete your paperwork as soon as possible after the disclosure. The details may be needed should a prosecution take place, so your paperwork must be accurate.

As a playworker, you should inform the designated child protection officer at your setting and take their advice and help. He or she will guide you through this difficult time. You must maintain confidentiality about the suspected abuse, and not discuss the details with anyone other than the designated person. If you feel that you need personal help, then ask for a counsellor to help you through this difficult and disturbing time.

How to help children and young people protect themselves

One way that playworkers can help to keep children and young people safe from personal and physical harm is to help them to protect themselves. Children can be equipped with the skills they need to help them to stay safe and, as a playworker, you are in a position to aid this process. It is important to recognise that children cannot always protect themselves, but they do have a right to be protected.

There are many ways that personal safety can be promoted by you as a playworker. Below are a few ideas and strategies that will help confirm your good practice and/or help you improve your practice:

- create an atmosphere where children feel safe and secure, and where they are listened to and valued
- have a range of caring adults whom children and staff can approach for help and advice
- be able to recognise signs and symptoms of possible abuse
- have clear procedures and lines of communication within the setting
- work closely with parents or carers and other professionals who care for children and young people
- attend child protection training and updates, and encourage other staff to do the same
- use play activities and opportunities to raise children or young people's awareness of self-protection issues and to help build confidence
- develop strategies to minimise the risk of abuse and allegations of abuse to both staff and children.

Protect children by helping them build self-confidence through play activities

CONSOLIDATION

1 If you have been involved in any instances of suspected abuse where a child or young person has made a disclosure to you, write about these. Remember to observe confidentiality at all times; any records you have completed will need to be kept at your setting but you may be able to show them to your assessor.

2 If you have not been involved in recognising abuse, read the following scenarios and explain what you would do in each situation when the child disclosed.

- Michael is 13 years old. He attends every session and often turns up very early. He never wears socks and his shoes have holes. His clothing is very old fashioned (obviously second-hand) and he never wears a coat, even in winter. He lives at home with his mum, who tends to drink heavily. Michael is always hungry and always volunteers to help with the tuck shop. The other children tend to buy him things or give him their change. One day he informs you that there is no food at home and that he hardly ever eats, only when his next door neighbour gives him food.

- Puja (aged 14 years) turns up every week at the youth club. She shows no interest whatsoever in boys. She wears baggy clothes. You notice during an activity that her stomach is very swollen. During discussions she admits that her periods have stopped.

- Sarah (aged 7 years) tells you that her babysitter (a neighbour's son) had a camera and wanted to take photographs of her in bed. At first Sarah let him, then he told her to lift up her nightdress. She did it. She later became frightened and started to cry so he gave her some sweets.

END OF UNIT TEST

1 Describe the common signs and indicators of physical, emotional, sexual abuse and neglect in children.

2 State how to distinguish between directly observed signs and indicators of abuse, other information and opinions, and why it is important to do so in any reports.

3 Explain the importance of responding promptly and calmly to a child's disclosure of abuse and how to do so.

4 State why it is important to communicate at the child's pace and not exert pressure on the child to disclose more than they wish.

Contribute to the work of your team

Unit A52

This unit is about the importance of playworkers being able to work well with others as part of a team. You will learn about the importance of effective team work, and how improving your own work and the work of your team can improve your organisation as a whole. This unit also covers examining your own actions and attitudes and considers the personal development opportunities that are available.

To fulfil your role as a playworker you must be able to work well with others as part of a team. This will enhance the quality of the service provided by the play setting. It will help provide a welcoming and friendly atmosphere where the children feel safe and secure. It will also reassure parents and carers that their children are being looked after by caring and professional playworkers.

This unit is divided into three elements:

- A52.1 Work effectively with your colleagues.
- A52.2 Improve your own work.
- A52.3 Help to improve the work of your organisation.

The Play Values covered in this unit are shown below:

Value No	Statement
1	The child must be at the centre of the process.
2	Play should empower a child or young person.
3	Play should be freely chosen and directed by the child or young person within the guidelines of the setting.
5	A play environment must be provided in which children feel physically and personally safe and able to take part in activities free from hazards.
6	Every child is an individual and should be respected for who they are.
7	As playworker, you should be considerate and caring.
8	As playworker, you should promote equal opportunities for all children and young people in your setting, regardless of ability, race, culture, social background, etc.
9	Within a play setting, you should be a positive role model and create co-operative working.
10	As playworker you should be comfortable working with children and others.
11	Play opportunities should be provided within the current legislative framework.
12	The play environment should be accessible to all.

A team is a group of people working together to achieve the same aims and objectives. We have teams for a variety of reasons, as you can see from the table below:

Reason for team	What the team does
To complete tasks	We can often achieve things we want to do as a team, which would have been more difficult to complete on our own
To help motivation	We often become more enthusiastic in groups
To keep up morale	By working together, we can support each other
To help others	We can help others by working collectively towards the same goal
To encourage people to feel at ease	We can discuss, take advice or just share opinions and ideas in a safe and secure forum
For security	To help with decisions and to work together towards polices and procedures
To increase individual skills and expertise	We all have different skills and, by working in a team, the quality of the provision we provide will be improved
To develop originality and resourcefulness	We can share ideas and skills and work together
To establish a consistent approach	A consistent approach helps to establish security for the children and young people

Within a team, people are given or assume a variety of roles. As a playworker, these may cover a wide range; they may be connected to your job description or they may be roles that you have taken on due to your skills, knowledge and/or interests. Within teams, people have different personalities and these guide people into different roles.

Team workers should have the following qualities:

- enthusiasm
- supportiveness
- sense of humour
- assertiveness
- respect
- ability to listen.

Each team needs to have an aim, i.e. an agreed purpose. People will take on roles in a team such as organiser, leader, etc. Whatever the role we have or adopt, we need to work to the best of our abilities.

✓ ACTIVE KNOWLEDGE

Think about your playwork team. What would be your team's aim? Who takes on which roles?

Enthusiastic person

Questioner

Uninterested person

Practical person

Self-conscious person

Uncooperative person

Talkative person

Academic person

Different people bring different skills to a team

What you need to learn

- How to establish good working relationships with your colleagues.
- The importance of clear communication.
- The purpose of team meetings.
- Procedures for dealing with conflict.

How to establish good working relationships with your colleagues

For a team to function well, they need:

- to communicate clearly with each other (including **written communication**)
- shared goals to achieve
- encouragement and guidance to achieve these goals
- to be supportive of each other.

Different members of the team may have different strengths and weaknesses. The members of the team may not always share the same points of view, but by working together and having discussions and debates, the best ways to do things will be decided. Playworkers need to listen to one another and share their points of view flexibly with others. You should have an open mind, respect other people's points of view and be prepared to support other people's ideas. This way you can all work together to achieve the same aims and goals, sharing the responsibilities and ensuring everything gets done.

The importance of effective teamwork is to ensure that children and young people are cared for in a secure and friendly environment, with consistency of care. All the staff should know what they and others are doing, and how this may affect their role. Where staff can share ideas and cooperate with each other, this will contribute to providing a safe environment for the children and young people. It will help to show that you respect each other.

A playworker needs to be friendly towards colleagues, offer to help and give assistance when necessary, and to share ideas. In an effective team, all members need to:

- communicate with others; listen to individual points of view with consideration
- have the confidence to seek support when they are not quite sure what to do
- be able to carry out any commitments they make; clarify these and inform other members so you all know what each other is doing and why
- know who to report problems to with regard to relationships in the team; you should speak with your **line manager** or supervisor if you have any problems and not gossip with other staff members because this could make things worse
- know, understand and share the team's aims; discuss these with your line manager and have a good understanding of what you are doing and how this meets the setting's aims

- distribute work fairly to meet individual skills, knowledge and ability and according to responsibility level
- acknowledge the strengths and weaknesses of others; we all have things we are good at or not so good at – by sharing the responsibilities the team will function well
- respect each other's beliefs, culture, background and views; be open-minded, try out new activities, be considerate of other people's beliefs and points of view.

An example of an out of school club policy, showing the club aims and objectives, is shown below.

The Calverton out-of-school club's aims

The aim of the Calverton out-of-school club is to provide a happy environment for children between the ages of 4 and 11 years.

To achieve these aims the staff must ensure that all children have a happy and rewarding time during their stay at the out of school club.

Aims and objectives

The overall aims of the Calverton out of school club are:
- to recruit and monitor high quality staff who met the needs of all children
- to encourage progress by providing a safe, nurturing and stimulating environment
- to generate a happy environment with warm and caring staff to provide total security for children and their parents
- to praise and recognise children's effort and achievement
- to equip children for the future by providing a framework of responsible behaviour
- to help children to develop life-long skills
- to enable working parents to be able to commit themselves to their career knowing that their children are happy, well cared for and stimulated.

If staff know you are reliable and trustworthy in whatever job you are doing – and that it will be done properly – then they will see you as a valuable member of the team. Trust is a very important part of teamwork; it comes from team members knowing they can depend on each other. As a team member, you need to be dependable and reliable. As playworkers, you must be honest enough to discuss any difficulties you have and to ask for help when you need it. You must believe that your colleagues will respond positively to your requests for help. At times, you will need to make sure you know exactly what you have to do, for example whether a child can drink water or milk. Always remember, if in doubt check it out. This will help to build on the team's strengths, as other team members will know that you are trustworthy.

In your job description, the person specification will usually include statements about working as a team (see overleaf).

Team working is important and contributes to the quality of experience the children receive because it ensures the smooth running of the setting. It maintains a friendly atmosphere, which helps the children feel happy and secure, and it reduces the possibility of conflict or a breakdown in communication. It is very important to carry out any agreed responsibilities to ensure the smooth running of the setting, to share the workloads and responsibilities and to reduce possible conflict. You should sort out your duties and responsibilities to ensure that everyone knows these in advance. Good working relationships with your colleagues means that you co-operate with each other, you tell each other what you are doing and why, and you follow the guidelines and policies of the setting.

ACTIVE KNOWLEDGE

Do you have set roles within your team?

Do you know who is responsible for carrying out the following?

Role	Responsible person
Collecting the children from school	
Showing children around the setting	
Answering the telephone	
Taking fees or subscriptions	
First aid	
Child protection issues	
Taking the register	
Petty cash	
Planning activities	
Supervising play activities	
Banking the money	
Calling team meetings	
Completing safety checks	
Answering the door	

The importance of clear communication

It is important to communicate clearly with your colleagues so that everyone knows and understands their role. They will then have a good idea of what you are doing and how this may relate to what they are doing. It will help the team members to work effectively with each other and the setting to run smoothly.

There are many ways that we communicate. Communication techniques are important and it may be that you use several at the same time, for example:

- body language – use eye-to-eye contact, stand at a sensible distance from the person you are communicating with
- speaking – speak clearly, do not use jargon
- listening – be an active listener, show you are listening by nodding and smiling, respond to what is said to you
- thinking – think before you speak
- facial expressions – show what you are thinking and feeling, be aware of the image you are trying to show.

Everyone in the team needs to follow the ground rules of the setting and communicate well with each other and the children and young people who use the setting. There are many important issues that team members must share with each other:

- discuss what activities are planned for the session and review them
- pass on messages and up-to-date information on what is happening
- support each other, especially in emergency situations
- encourage each other, be constructive with **feedback**
- when there is conflict in the team it needs to be handled delicately – try not to take sides
- give your opinion honestly.

A playworker should know how to communicate with the managers in their organisation. This should be with respect, openly and honestly. You can do this formally, for example at team meetings and interviews, or informally at the beginning or end of the session. You may also have an appraisal with your manager (see page 155).

It is important to carry out your duties as agreed or warn colleagues in good time if you cannot do this. Your team members will be relying on you to complete the agreed duties, for example the adult–child ratio may not be correct if you do not attend your place of work and temporary cover may have to be arranged, which will take some planning. If you vary your responsibilities and duties, you should only do so with the agreement of your colleagues and line manager. This will ensure sufficient staff ratios, prevent errors and avoid confusion and conflict.

There are many situations in which you may have to provide information to your colleagues, for example if parents inform you that their child will not be attending the session for the rest of the week. However, you should not provide colleagues with information if you are dealing with a confidential matter relating to a child or their family, e.g. a child protection issue. Remember, it is very important to maintain confidentiality. Your colleagues may be aware that there is an issue, but the details must not be shared.

The purpose of team meetings

Each team in which you work should hold regular meetings. They will be held for different purposes and could be informal, e.g. at the end of a session, or held more formally at a set time on a regular basis. Team meetings can involve the whole team or just part of the team depending on the issues to be discussed. There are many reasons why you might hold team meetings, as shown in the spider diagram below.

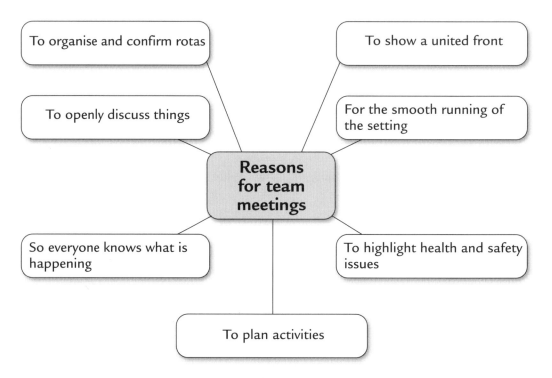

Regular team meetings should have an agenda, and all team members can submit items (see below).

Weekly team meeting agenda
1 Welcome and apologies
2 Matters arising from last meeting
3 Review of the week
4 Planning for the next week

Team discussions are important for the following reasons, and playworkers should try to contribute to them:

- it is important to keep colleagues up-to-date and informed of progress
- to ensure the safety of the setting, the staff and the children
- to find out what is working and what is not and to avoid errors and conflict
- if the team works well together, the play setting usually runs smoothly
- good communication ensures that staff feel valued

- planning shared by the whole team ensures a calm, organised play setting with a consistent approach.

Procedures for dealing with conflict

Conflict within teams can occur for a variety of reasons, e.g. someone not doing their share of the work or a disagreement between staff members. Solving conflict often means negotiating.

When conflict occurs it is important that it should not disrupt the work of a team. Other team members should not be drawn in or become involved. A professional and pleasant atmosphere should be ensured for the smooth running of the setting. Conflict can sometimes be resolved by compromise. This shows respect and understanding of other people's views; it helps maintain good relationships and promotes effective teamwork. You can support colleagues who are involved in conflict by:

- not taking sides
- being non-judgemental
- listening to both sides
- quoting your policy and procedures
- explaining where they can seek further help.

Conflict happens all the time. Little problems that are not dealt with can become big problems so need dealing with promptly. When faced with conflict in the team, you should:

- communicate calmly
- deal with the problems as they arise
- have a positive approach
- listen carefully to the other person's point of view.

It is important to support and help each other in times of conflict.

ACTIVE KNOWLEDGE

1 Jane is new to your team. She has just been appointed as an assistant playworker and is to start her job next Monday. She asks you about the team.

What do you say, and what do you not say?

2 Two colleagues are disagreeing about whether the setting should allow children to use roller blades in the outside play area. The argument is becoming very heated and you are called over to give your opinion.

State what you would do and why.

3 Imagine you have a disagreement with another worker about a game they are playing with the children. You think the game is unsuitable. Before you have a chance to explain your reasoning, your line manager calls you into the office and asks you to write a report about the incident.

Write your own report.

4 You overhear two colleagues (one volunteer and one casual worker) talking about a new female member of staff. You overhear the volunteer say the only reason she got the job is because she is black.

What would you do and say?

CONSOLIDATION

1 Recall an instance when you worked effectively with other team members. It could have been planning an activity, planning an outing or doing a hygiene task. Record it on a diary sheet.

2 Complete a witness statement about how you established working relationships with colleagues and how you have maintained these relationships. Remember to include your reasons for doing what you did.

3 Reflect on a team meeting that you have attended. Explain your contribution. You could include the agenda and the minutes in your work.

Improve your own work

What you need to learn

- How to **evaluate** your work.
- Self-evaluation and self-assessment.
- Dealing with criticism.
- Appraisals and personal development plans.

How to evaluate your work

In order to work well as a team member, you should be able to improve your own work as a playworker by evaluating what you do. You need to be able to work out what you already do that is good, and seek to change the things that you don't do so well.

To become effective in your role as a playworker, it is vital that you develop your own knowledge and practice. This will be a continuous circle, as shown below.

If you feel the need to criticise another team member, remember:

- try to raise the issue with the person concerned
- get someone to act as a mediator
- try not to be too condemning
- criticise the action not the person.

Young children learn initially by copying and trying things out. As a playworker, you can also learn in a similar way; if you see a good idea, try it out (or even copy it). If you want to be good at something that someone else can do well, ask them about it. Watch them at their work and then try to follow their good example. By improving your practice in line with up-to-date developments and legislation, you will develop your competence as a playworker. You will gain a better understanding of your own role and responsibilities in the areas where you work.

It is the role and responsibility of each member of staff to monitor, evaluate and improve their own and others' performance. There are a variety of methods you could use to do this. The methods you choose will depend on your preferences and the opportunities available at your setting.

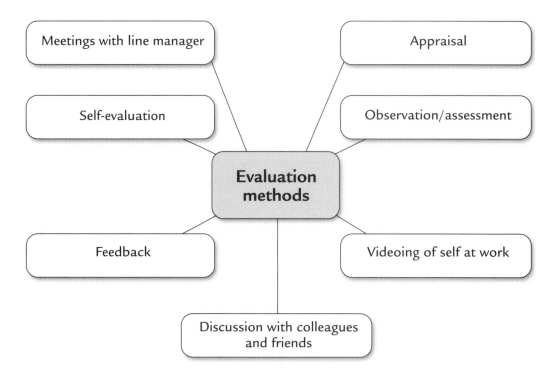

Self-evaluation and self-assessment

Self-evaluation

Self-evaluation involves taking a critical look at yourself. It is always a good starting point for your evaluation. You will need to think about:

- your own personality
- your values
- your priorities
- your interests.

Think about it

Consider the picture below.

1 Can you relate to any of these values, priorities and interests?

2 Draw a picture to represent your own values, priorities and interests.

Your values, priorities and interests will impact on your practice even though you may not always be aware of this. For example:

- Did your parents instil in you the importance of good table manners? Do you think this is important for the children and young people in your care?
- Do you pay all your bills as they arrive? If so, how do you feel when parents do not pay fees on time? Are you judgemental about them?

Self-assessment

It is important to self-assess your work and get feedback from colleagues. In this way, you will be able to identify your strengths and weaknesses. This is called being a reflective practitioner. You can reflect on your work, highlight examples of good practice and improve your performance where possible. This will help by:

- allowing any issue to be addressed before problems occur
- identifying your training needs
- helping you to see things from other people's points of view.

Being a reflective practitioner involves looking back on past performances and identifying things that were good and things that perhaps did not go so well. Use this information to improve your performance in the future.

It is important to identify potential failures as well as successes and actual failures. This is for the following reasons:

- to avoid actual failure (things not working out correctly) in the future
- to improve working practice
- to prevent unsafe situations occurring
- to avoid conflicts, e.g. people falling out because their views are not being listened to
- to maintain good staff morale; people lose confidence when things go wrong.

Once you have opened your mind and challenged yourself, you need to take note of constructive thoughts and comments that are based on value judgements. This will ensure progressive learning, especially if you can identify, adjust and challenge your own personal thoughts and practice. This can be achieved by discussing and debating values and attitudes. Self-evaluation and self-assessment affect the continuous development of playworkers by:

- identifying strengths and weaknesses
- developing confidence and boosting self-esteem
- raising self-awareness
- allowing issues to be addressed before they become a problem
- constantly improving performance
- allowing you to see things from other people's points of view
- becoming more open and receptive to other people's points of view
- improving performance and raising standards in the play setting
- identifying training needs
- making you more approachable
- helping you to take on further responsibilities with confidence.

The reasons why it is important to continuously improve your practice in the play setting are shown in the table below.

For the children	For the organisation	For yourself
Children's enjoyment Children feel secure Welfare of the children	Keeps you up-to-date on new issues Maintains high standards Sets a good example to new staff	Boosts your self-esteem and confidence Identifies your strengths and weaknesses Gives you ideas and pointers for improvement

Below is a diagram of a reflective learning cycle; you could use this to change situations you are not happy with.

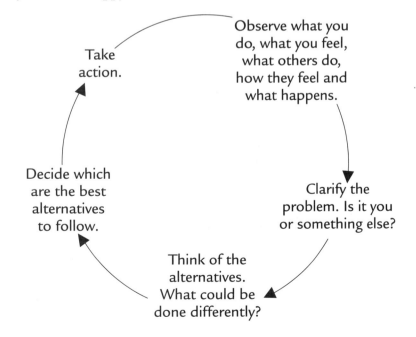

Take action.

Observe what you do, what you feel, what others do, how they feel and what happens.

Clarify the problem. Is it you or something else?

Think of the alternatives. What could be done differently?

Decide which are the best alternatives to follow.

1 Are there situations or people you avoid because you are not sure how to handle or deal with them? Perhaps if you think about these situations carefully you could identify some of the reasons, make changes and review the situation.

2 Identify what you are good at and why. Identify what you are not good at and why. Think about some of the reasons why things don't go as well as expected. These reasons could be considered blockages. One of these blockages could be your reluctance to ask for help or advice. You may believe that asking shows people that you don't know the answer, and you may not want them to know this. You may feel embarrassed about not knowing something (because you think you should). Not knowing may lead to a dangerous situation arising. You *do* have the right to know the answers to your questions.

3 Think of a time you asked someone a question and got the brush off. What did you do? Did you:
   a) apologise for having bothered them
   b) walk away and try to find the answer yourself
   c) explain that you need the information to do your job.

If your answer is **c**, then you are assertive. If you answered with either **a** or **b** then you could become more assertive. Remember, you have the right to know the answer. If these situations happen again, try to be more assertive about asking for the information you need; practise this to yourself, so you know you can do it.

Dealing with criticism

There are many ways that people criticise others within a team. Any criticism should always be done in a positive manner with awareness of the feelings of others. To receive criticism is sometimes very hard, but if it will improve your practice and the quality of care and provision you provide, then it is important.

People need to be able to help you improve your skills; to do this they need to give you their honest opinion. This may not be easy for you to hear to begin with, but it will help in the long run. If you can listen to what people say and take their criticism positively, you will be receptive to new ideas, raise your standards, improve your practice and become more approachable to other staff, children and their parents. This is called handling criticism positively and it is important for the following reasons:

- it indicates maturity
- it makes you receptive to new ideas
- it shows you can accept your faults and improve on them
- it raises standards
- it encourages team work and raises staff morale
- staff, children and parents will feel that you are approachable.

We all need reassurance that we are doing a good job. Sometimes we require more than this; we need help to recognise and face a problem and then deal with it. In order to carry out your job properly, you need to be supported by a management structure that will care for your wellbeing, listen to you and help you to develop.

Appraisals and personal development plans

Within your setting, there will be a senior colleague or line manager with whom you can discuss your own issues, both personal and professional. You will also have a formal meeting at regular intervals (once/twice a year) in which views and opinions regarding your performance are formally recorded. This is called an appraisal, and it should take place on regular basis and be confidential.

Appraisals are important for the following reasons:

- they aid your personal development
- they give everyone space to air their views
- they provide an opportunity to think through new ideas
- they sort out personal grievances
- they help the setting to run smoothly
- they make people feel valued
- they help people to focus on their **future responsibilities** and career moves
- they build on support and supervision sessions.

Being honest during your appraisal will help to build trust and respect

During your appraisal you should be open and honest. This is important because:

- you will be unable to progress, develop or make improvements if you don't know what the problems are
- without frankness and honesty, the appraisal process would be worthless
- it will create trust and respect
- it will build relationships between yourself and others.

During your appraisal, you can discuss many things; the table below shows the types of things you may discuss.

	Very good	Good	Fair	Requires improvement	Comments
Attendance					I have been off work only once when I had the flu
Punctuality					I am always on time, except when the bus is late
Activity planning					I don't always have everything ready
Communication with colleagues					I find my colleagues supportive, they are very experienced
Communication with children					I enjoy this part of the job
Communication with parents					I don't have much opportunity to speak to parents, my co-ordinator usually does this
Working in a team					I try to help my colleagues
Playing with children					I really like to play when invited
Awareness of health and safety issues					I think I need training about the legal side of health and safety

The appraisal will help you to highlight any **training and development needs** that you have. Once you have identified your development needs, you can complete a personal development plan similar to the one at the top of page 157.

Personal development plan

Date: *22 February 2003*

Name: *Margaret Smith*

Date of next appraisal: *22 August 2003*

Area for development	Action	Timescale
Activity planning	Plan in advance some activities. Use set form for guidance to help ensure all equipment and materials are ready. Put forward activity plans at staff meetings so they go on the programme of events and opportunities. Attend training at the local play forum.	To start immediately
Health and safety	Manager to check courses available locally and to ensure funding from management fund/Early Years Partnership.	To discuss at next appraisal
My practice	Undertake NVQ Level 2, discuss progress at each appraisal session.	Ongoing
Different cultures and practices	Manager to put purchasing more equipment/materials/ reference books on agenda at staff meeting. To attend training at local Play Forum on celebrating festivals.	Next staff meeting in April

Personal development can be established by a range of methods (see below), some of which you may have identified during your appraisal or from your personal development plan.

Method	Example	How to access
Short courses	First aid Basic food hygiene Basic counselling Lifting and handling Child protection	Local further education college Local play forum Internet
Workshops	Craft activities Festivals Outdoor play	Local play forum
Visits	Other play settings Play forums	Local directory (Early Years Partnership)
National regional training	NVQ in Playwork	Sprito Local further education college National Play Council Local training providers
Academic qualifications	GCSEs A Levels	Local further education college Community college
Research	Types of craft activities Articles on medical conditions	Internet Local library
Talking to other playworkers	Playworkers or support groups Regional playwork meetings	Play development workers Play forums
Exchanging roles	Swop with another playworker	Local directory Support meetings

✓ Find an article that may have some value to you as a playworker, then complete the review sheet below.

Type of review: video / TV programme / book / article

Title: Topic:

Publisher: Length:

Brief synopsis:

How it could relate to my practice:

Personal learning:

Name: Date: Signature:

Learning is a continuous process, involving formal and informal learning, linked to both our job roles and our personal development. It is important for several reasons:

- it means you are constantly updating your skills
- it stops you losing ambition
- it builds on your knowledge
- it makes you more enthusiastic
- it increases your motivation
- it betters your career possibilities.

CONSOLIDATION

1 Complete a personal development plan and discuss this with your line manager.

2 Draw a flow chart to show the progression routes and courses that will help to improve your skills and knowledge in playwork. Include copies of certificates of recent and relevant training that you have participated in.

Help to improve the work of your organisation

What you need to learn

- How to improve your work.
- Why it is important to listen to feedback.
- How to act on suggestions for improving services.

How to improve your work

Improving your work is an on-going process for playworkers. It has personal benefits but also enhances the quality of the service you provide. To continually evaluate and improve your work is important because:

- it helps you maintain high standards because you are aware of what people require
- it improves the care and welfare of the children and young people, helping them to feel cared for and respected in a child centred environment
- it keeps you and the other staff updated on new issues, e.g. legislation, identifying good practice and following it through
- it makes all staff feel valued and able to suggest improvements
- it gives parents confidence in the setting.

The organisation of your practice influences the effectiveness of what is achieved in the play setting:

- if the staff team works well together the play setting usually runs smoothly because everyone knows their role and responsibilities
- good communication ensures that staff feel valued
- planning that is shared by the whole team ensures a calm, organised play setting where activities are carried out and evaluated to monitor their success or failure
- effective organisational policies ensure staff are aware of the correct procedures; everyone knows what is expected of them
- good teamwork and effective policies create a safe, calm, happy and healthy environment for everyone.

There are many ways in which the work of the team can be improved, as shown in the table overleaf.

Method	Example
Discussion with staff	Staff meetings
Planning and organising	Effective planning of staff work rotas and activities
Training	Information on relevant training courses
Atmosphere	Creating a warm and friendly atmosphere
Effective communication	Meeting formally and informally to share information and ideas
Policies	Clear and relevant policies that all staff are aware of and implement
Activities	A range of challenging and stimulating activities with enthusiastic staff
Parental involvement	Meetings, open evenings, fund raising events
Evaluation	Set time aside to discuss potential failures, successes and actual failures
Feedback	A range of methods to receive feedback from participants and others

Each team will choose methods to help improve their practice and these will depend on the individual setting and what is most appropriate in that setting. Identifying things that went well and that were not so successful will help improve the working practice. It will help you to raise the standard of care and avoid conflict, thus making a more stable environment. It is also very good for staff morale, and will help avoid unsafe situations occurring.

Staff evaluation affects the continuous development of playworkers in the following ways:
- it identifies strengths and weaknesses
- it develops confidence and boosts self-esteem
- it raises self-awareness
- it allows issues to be addressed before they become a problem
- it constantly improves performances
- it helps you to see things from other points of view
- self-awareness makes you more open and receptive to others
- improving performance raises standards in the play setting
- it identifies training needs
- it makes you more approachable
- it helps you take on further responsibilities with confidence.

There are many contributions you can make to the evaluation process, which include the following:
- share your ideas, then people know what you are thinking and don't have to guess
- ask other people for ideas – they can share their past experiences, which may help you to gain more detailed knowledge of what works and why
- participate fully in team meetings – you will feel part of the team, understand what is happening and why, and be involved in planning for the next week
- devise questionnaires to see what improvements can be made

- be approachable – people are more likely to share their personal thoughts with you if you are friendly, ask what they think and listen to their ideas
- be observant – you can learn a lot by watching colleagues and seeing what works and why.

Why it is important to listen to feedback

Feedback can be obtained from several areas, as shown below.

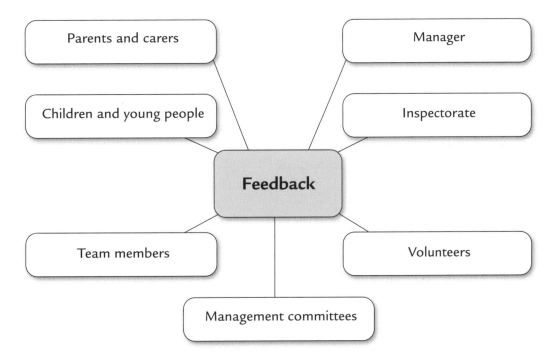

Because they benefit from the service on offer, children and parents or carers will have important knowledge that they can offer as feedback. They can give a continuous flow of information particularly if a suggestion box is available. This will mean that their needs and issues can be addressed quickly.

You can ask parents and carers for feedback on the services they receive by:

- parent meetings – inviting parents to a meeting to discuss issues and share their points of view
- a suggestion box – leave this out in clear view, with paper available for people to write down their suggestions for activities or improvements; take suggestions seriously and give them the consideration they require
- individual discussions – these can be informal, e.g. at the end of an activity or when you are working with children and young people
- asking them to complete a questionnaire.

Areas on which feedback about the services you provide could be obtained include those shown below.

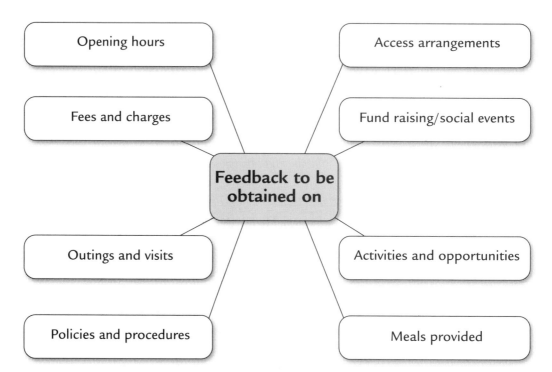

Feedback from children and young people using the facilities can also provide a useful tool for improving your practice. You could use some of the suggestions listed above, but also include evaluations by children and young people of the services and activities they experience. An example of a feedback sheet is shown on page 163.

Whatever method you use to obtain feedback, children and young people should be listened to and their ideas and opinions discussed, so that they are aware of the positive and negative implications of their suggestions.

When receiving feedback, you should always be objective. Do not take it personally but see how it can improve your practice. It is important to listen to parents and carers' feedback so you can provide the best service possible. If parents and carers are not happy, they may remove their children from the setting. You could cater more to their individual tastes if you have received some feedback on how happy they are with the services provided. Receiving feedback is important to ensure that everyone feels a sense of belonging and that their input is valued.

Activity: _____

Age: _____ Gender: Male ☐ Female ☐

Please colour in the face that represents how you felt and tick the yes/no boxes.

Were the instructions easy to follow?   Yes ☐ No ☐

Was the activity interesting?   Yes ☐ No ☐

Had you done this activity before?   Yes ☐ No ☐

Was there enough room?   Yes ☐ No ☐

Was there enough materials/equipment?   Yes ☐ No ☐

Did you enjoy what you did?   Yes ☐ No ☐

Would you like to do/play this again?   Yes ☐ No ☐

Now tell us how you think it could be improved:

Thank you for completing this form.

How to act on suggestions for improving services

If you ask for feedback, you must be prepared to act on suggestions and try out or revise what has been put forward. You should also provide feedback on the suggestions you have not acted on. Each setting will have ways of improving its practice. Playworkers should be open minded and willing to try out new ideas, and set procedures should be in place to ensure this. Before changes are made, however, you will need to ensure that they are safe, realistic and positive for the setting. You will need to ask yourself, do they adhere to the safety policies of the setting? You could then try out the new idea but monitor it closely and make changes as necessary.

You will need to keep everyone informed and involved in any changes made. You could have trial periods for new ideas and then re-assess their effect. The team must use effective planning within the limitations of the setting and take funding and legislation into account.

ACTIVE KNOWLEDGE

What action would your setting take to share and discuss a suggestion for improvement?

Before implementing a new idea, it is important to discuss any suggestions with colleagues and to take account of their ideas. By having discussions with your colleagues and listening to their points of view, you can decide on the best way to approach the suggestions. Your colleagues may have experience of the best way to put things into practice.

When changes are implemented there are procedures to follow to provide colleagues and managers with feedback. These include the following:

- a team meeting to inform team members of changes
- relevant resources or training if needed
- written reports
- informal feedback at the end of the session
- effective ongoing communication.

It is important to make sure that monitoring and evaluation of the implemented idea is complete and factual:

- otherwise weaknesses will not be acknowledged and changes will not be forthcoming
- otherwise you could create a negative working environment
- because if it is incomplete you may miss out on important issues that need addressing
- because it would be a waste of time if the process was not complete and factual
- otherwise strengths may not be acknowledged and weaknesses may not be addressed.

CONSOLIDATION

1 Recall a time when you have:
- made a suggestion (to improve practice)
- taken up another person's suggestion
- involved children, parents or carers in making suggestions.

2 Design a questionnaire and send it out to help improve your practice. Explain what you did and why. Remember to use open questions in your questionnaire.

3 Make a flow chart to show the procedures of your setting for receiving and implementing suggestions to improve practice.

END OF UNIT TEST

1 Describe the ways in which you can establish **effective working relationships** with your colleagues.

2 List some situations in which you may need help in your work and why you should always ask for help and information in those particular situations.

3 State why it is important to assess your own work yourself and get feedback from your colleagues.

4 Explain what it means to 'handle criticism positively' and why this is important.

5 List the types of situations in which customers give you feedback on the services they receive.

6 Why is it important to listen to customers' feedback?

Further reading

Accident Prevention in Daycare and Play Settings, Kate Gilbert, Child Accident Prevention Trust.

Good Practice in Playwork, Paul Bonel and Jennie Lindon, Sprito.

Growing Up: 8–Young Adulthood, Jennie Lindon, National Children's Bureau.

Guidelines of good practice for out of school care, Kids Club Network.

Involving Volunteers in Children's Play, Donne Buck, Volunteer Centre, UK.

Parachute Play, Meynell, Meynell Games Publications.

Partnership with Parents, Phillipa Russell, National Children's Bureau.

Play and Care Out of School, Pat Petrie, HMSO.

Playwork, Annie Davy, Macmillan Press.

Resource books for parents of children and young people with disabilities, 10–18-years-old, Council for Disabled Children.

The Excellence of Play, Janet Moyles, Open University Press.

Your Child from 5 to 11, Jennie Lindon, National Children's Bureau.

Glossary

Acceptable level of challenge and risk:
– a level of challenge and risk that provides the potential forchildren and young people to learn and develop without causing risks that are not acceptable to your play setting's policies and procedures for health and safety.

Additional needs:
– disabilities, physical, educational, emotional or behavioural needs.

Agreed policies and procedures:
– the policies and procedures of the play setting, the wider organisation and/or relevant laws.

Anti-discriminatory practice:
– taking positive action to counter discrimination; this will involve identifying and challenging discrimination and being positive in your playwork practice about people's differences.

Appropriate behaviour:
– behaviour that demonstrates that the child is respected and valued; behaviour that is not abusive or derogatory to the child, either physically, emotionally or sexually.

Assessing risk:
– your organisation should already have carried out formal risk assessments for all aspects of your play setting; this will result in written health and safety policies and procedures; however, every worker is responsible for identifying hazards when they occur, assessing the risks they present and taking action to control these risks in line with his or her organisation's policies and procedures.

Behavioural signs and indicators of abuse:
– behaviour which is unusual for the child's age or stage of development, for example precocious sexual behaviour or knowledge, or an unusual fear of adults or other children.

Casualty:
– the person, child or adult, who has suffered the injury or illness.

Colleagues:
– the people you work with, people working at the same level as yourself or your manager(s).

Confidential information:
– information that should only be shared with people who have a right to have it, for example your team leader, supervisor or manager (not other children and young people or parents/carers).

Creative play:	– play that is inventive and/or productive, e.g. writing, construction, artwork or music.
Cultural background:	– attitudes, values, beliefs, traditions and sometimes language which make one community different to another; examples include Catholic or Protestant communities in areas where this makes a major difference, children and young people in traveller communities or children and young people from ethnic minorities.
Cultural play:	– play which involves and/or raises awareness of different cultures and their values and practices.
Disclosure of abuse:	– the child telling someone about abuse they are experiencing or have experienced in the past.
Effective working relationships:	– the type of relationship with your colleagues that helps the team to work well and provide a high level of service to the customer. This includes getting along well with your colleagues, being fair to them, avoiding unnecessary disagreements and not letting your personal life influence the way you relate to colleagues.
Emergency services:	– usually the ambulance service.
Emergency:	– any situation that immediately threatens the health and safety of children, staff or yourself.
Emotional abuse:	– another person, an adult or child, hurting the child emotionally, for example, by taunting, bullying, threatening or discriminating against them.
Environmental play:	– play which involves and/or raises awareness of natural elements and/or wildlife and their survival.
Evaluate:	– thinking about your work and identifying what you do well and what you could improve in.
Feedback:	– other people, customers or colleagues, telling you what they think.
Future responsibilities:	– these could be new duties that you want to take on or new duties that your line manager wants to give you – this could include promotion.
Ground rules:	– agreed rules for a play opportunity; this will usually cover issues such as behaviour, health and safety, co-operation, respect or other issues requested by the children and young people.
Hazard:	– something that may cause harm to the health, safety and welfare of users of the play setting, for example, broken glass, faulty play equipment, doors left open that should be closed.

Hazardous substances:	– these could include, for example, certain types of paints, correcting fluids, glue. The manufacturer should provide information on any hazards and how the substances should be used and what to do in an emergency.
Health and safety policies and procedures:	– these will be written policies and procedures developed by your organisation in line with relevant legislation, such as the Health and Safety at Work Act, the Children Act and Control of Substances Hazardous to Health regulations.
Health, safety and welfare incidents:	– these would include situations where someone was actually harmed but should also include situations where a person could easily have been harmed.
Hygiene hazards:	– include dirty or unhygienic toilets, washing facilities or kitchens, unsafe practices when preparing and serving food and drinks, dog mess in outdoor areas.
Imaginative play:	– play that involves 'pretend' roles or acting out fantasy situations.
Individuality:	– the way that everyone is different from everyone else for example because of their appearance, attitudes, behaviour.
Line manager:	– the manger or supervisor to whom you report.
Missing persons:	– for example, children going missing during play sessions.
Neglect:	– the child who does not receive a level of care sufficient for him or her to develop in the same way as other children of his/her age and stage of development.
Organisation's policies and procedures:	– what your organisation says its staff should and should not do in certain situations.
Other information:	– about the child, for example information that an injury has been caused accidentally during play.
Other people involved:	– these may be other members of staff or other children or staff apart from the casualty.
Partial disclosure:	– the child only partly telling someone about abuse.
People with particular needs:	– people with disabilities or medical conditions which may mean they need special attention following accidents and emergencies.
Physical abuse:	– another person, an adult or child, hurting the child physically.
Physical play:	– play that is physically active, for example football, rounders or tag.

Physical signs and indicators of abuse:	– injuries not consistent with age related play; other reasonable accidental injuries or physical signs of neglect.
Play cues:	– facial expressions, language or body language that communicate a child or young person's wish to play or invite others to play.
Play environment:	– environments with resources that stimulate the child or young person to play.
Play opportunity:	– any type of resource or activity that provides the children or young people with opportunities to play.
Play setting:	– anywhere where children and young people play, for example, an indoor play centre or adventure playground.
Positive behaviour:	– for example co-operating; helping; encouraging others; treating others fairly; being unselfish; comforting others; and other ways of responding positively to the feelings of others.
Positive relationships:	– relationships that benefit the children and young people; and the children and young people's ability to participate in and benefit from play.
Qualified assistance:	– someone who has a recognised first aid qualification or the emergency services.
Relevant laws:	– laws that are relevant to a play setting, such as the Health and Safety at Work Act, Control of Substances Hazardous to Health regulations, the Children Act.
Requirements of your organisation:	– the procedures and policies of your play setting as they apply to children and young people's rights, health and safety.
Resources:	– equipment and materials that will stimulate play. These materials include natural materials (such as earth, water, sand, clay or wood); construction materials (such as blocks); computer and IT equipment; communication resources (resources to support speaking, listening, reading and writing); 'loose parts' (items that can be moved from place to place, carried, rolled, lifted, piled one on top of the other or combined to create new structures or experiences); real tools (such as carpentry or cooking equipment); bikes, trolleys, swings, climbing structures and ropes; paints, drawing equipment, modelling and fabrics; music, colours, scientific and mathematical equipment (such as clocks and calendars); dressing-up materials, mirrors, cameras, videos to enable children to

	explore their own identity; items or experiences (such as poetry and literature) that allow for reflection about abstract concepts.
Risk:	– the likelihood of a hazard actually causing harm to children, young people and others; this will often be influenced by the age or stage of development of the children and young people involved.
Security hazards:	– for example strangers and opportunities for younger children to leave a supervised setting.
Sexual abuse:	– another person, an adult or child, using the child for sexual purposes.
Social background:	– family circumstances in terms of employment, income and education.
Team discussions:	– these will usually be team meetings but could include more informal discussions with team members and line managers.
Training and development:	– this could involve going on a course, but would also include watching other members of staff doing things that are new to you, receiving instructions from other members of staff on new things you have to do and having the opportunity to practise new skills.
Written communication:	– this could involve short notes, memos, letters or other informal documents.

Useful addresses

Every effort has been made to ensure that all details were up to date at the time of publication.

Many of the details below are for each organisation's head office, which should be able to provide local contact numbers.

ADD/ADHD Family Support Group
1a The High Street
Dilton Marsh
Nr Westbury
Wilts BA13 4DL

Barnardo's
Tanners Lane
Barkingside
Ilford
Essex IG6 1QG
Tel: 020 8550 8822
Web: www.barnardos.org.uk

British Allergy Foundation
Deepdene House
30 Bellgrove Road
Welling
Kent DA16 3PY
Tel: 020 8303 8525
Web: www.allergyfoundation.com

British Council of Disabled People
Litchurch Plaza
Litchurch Lane
Derby DE24 8AA
Tel: 01332 295551
Minicom: 01332 295581
Fax: 01332 295580
Web: www.bcodp.org.uk

British Deaf Association
1–3 Worship Street
London EC2A 2AB
Text phone: 020 7588 3529
Video phone: 020 7496 9539
Voice phone: 020 7588 3520
Web: www.bda.org.uk

British Red Cross Society (BRCS)
10th Floor Westminster Tower
3 Albert Embankment
London SE1 7SX
Training tel: 020 7388 8777
Web: www.redcross.org.uk

Child Accident Prevention Trust (CAPT)
18–20 Farringdon Lane
London EC1R 3AU
Tel: 020 7608 3828
Web: www.capt.org.uk

ChildLine
Studd Street
London N1 0QW
Helpline: 0800 1111
Web: www.childline.org.uk

Children's Society
Edward Rudolf House
Margery Street
London WC1X 0JL
Tel: 020 7841 4436
Web: www.the-childrens-society.org.uk

Commission for Racial Equality
Elliot House
10–12 Allington Street
London SW1E 5EH
Tel: 0207 828 7022
Fax: 0207 630 7605
Email: info@cre.gov.uk
Web: www.cre.gov.uk

Council for Awards in Children's Care and Education (CACHE)
8 Chequer Street
St Albans
Herts AL1 3XZ
Tel: 01727 847636 or 867333
Fax: 01727 867609
Web: www.cache.org.uk

CRUSE Bereavement Care
126 Sheen Road
Richmond
Surrey TW9 1UR
Tel: 020 8939 9530
Helpline: 0870 1671677
Web: www.crusebereavementcare.org.uk

EPOCH (End all Physical Punishment of Children)
77 Holloway Road
London N7 8JZ
Tel: 020 7700 0627
Associated website:www.stophitting.com

Kidscape
2 Grosvenor Gardens
London SW1W 0DH
Tel: 020 7730 3300
Fax: 020 7730 7081
Email: webinfo@kidscape.org.uk
Web: www.kidscape.org.uk/

MIND (National Association for Mental Health)
15–19 Broadway
London E15 4BQ
Tel: 020 8519 2122
Fax: 020 8519 21725
Email: contact@mind.org.uk
Web: www.mind.org.uk

National Childminding Association (NCMA)
8 Masons Hill
Bromley
Kent BR2 9EY
Tel: 020 8464 6164
Fax: 020 8290 6834
Email: info@ncma.org.uk
Web: www.ncma.org.uk

National Deaf Children's Society
15 Dufferin Street
London
EC1Y 8UR
Tel: 020 7490 8656
Email: ndcs@ndcs.org.uk
Web: www.ndcs.org.uk

National Drugs Helpline
Helpline: 0800 77 66 00
Email: helpline@ndh.org.uk
Web: www.ndh.org.uk

NSPCC (National Society for the Prevention of Cruelty to Children)
42 Curtain Road
London EC2A 3NH
Tel: 020 7825 2500
Fax: 020 7825 2525
Helpline: 0808 800 5000
Textphone: 0800 056 0566
Web: www.nspcc.org.uk

National Toy and Leisure Libraries
68 Churchway
London NW1 1LT
Tel: 020 7387 9592
Fax: 020 7383 2714
Email: admin@natll.ukf.net
Web: www.natll.org.uk

Royal Society for the Prevention of Accidents (RoSPA)
Edgbaston Park
353 Bristol Road
Edgbaston
Birmingham B5 7ST
Tel: 0121 248 2000
Email: help@rospa.co.uk
Web: www.rospa.co.uk

SCOPE
6 Market Road
London N7 9PW
Helpline: 0800 800 333
Email: cphelpline@scope.org.uk
Web: www.scope.org.uk

St. John Ambulance
27 St John's Lane
London EC1M 4BU
Tel: 08700 10 49 50
Email: info@sja.org.uk
Web: www.sja.org.uk

Index

A

abuse *see* child abuse
accident book   105
accidents   97–113
   accident book   105
   minor   97–8
   recording   104–8
   reporting   104–8
ACE CLUB mnemonic   21
ACPC (Area Child Protection Committee)   117
addresses   179–80
appraisals   155–8
Area Child Protection Committee (ACPC)   117
assumptions   x

B

behaviour
   acceptable and unacceptable   5
   challenging   5, 24–8
   changes   126
   encouraging positive 16–9
   ground rules   53
   unwanted   24, 25
body language   141
boisterous play   93
boundaries of activity 88–9
boundaries, importance 19–23

C

carers *see* parents for relevant items
casualty protection   100–4
CE mark   76
child abuse   115–38
   disclosure   133–8
   importance of recording 131–3

predisposing factors 129–30
   recognising   129–30
reporting signs of possible abuse   120–8
signs of   116, 120–8
child-centred environment 42
child protection   115–38
Child Protection Framework 117
child protection policies 118, 130–1
Children Act (1989) 2, 28–9, 54, 66, 75, 77, 116–7
close supervision   92
communication skills
   different ages   10–11
   listening   7–9
complaints procedure   32–3
confidential information   3–4
confidentiality statement   3
conflict management   24–8
constant supervision   92
contacts   179–80
Control of Substances Hazardous to Health and Safety Regulations (2003, COSHH)   75
COSHH (Control of Substances Hazardous to Health and Safety Regulations, 2003)   75
creative achievement   38
creative play   40
cultural play   40

D

Data Protection Act (1998)   3
departing children from the setting   65
development experiences 37–40

DfES (Department for Education and Skills)   2
disclosure
   full   133
   legal obligation to tell others   135
   partial   133
   responding appropriately 134–6
   responding promptly   134
discrimination
   countering   13–5
   parents, effect on   31–2

E

emergency   97–113
   contact information 106–7
   evacuation procedure 111–2, 112–3
   fire   109, 110, 111–3
   missing persons   110
   procedures   109–10
   security incidents   110
   services, when to call   104
   situations   100–4
emotional abuse   116, 128
emotional development   23
emotional needs   5
emotional stability   38
encouraging children   13
ending play sessions   61–7
environment creation for play 41–6
environmental play   40
Equal opportunities policy 4–5
equipment safety standards 76–8
equipment, new   89
evacuation procedure 111–2, 112–3
experimentation play   37
exploration play   37